Praise
Unaf

"Susie Davis invites us into her own story with grace and hospitality, tenderness and courage. If you've ever been overwhelmed by fear, you'll be so thankful for the way Susie takes you by the hand and leads you to a better way of living."

—SHAUNA NIEQUIST, author of *Bread & Wine*

"Don't pick up *Unafraid* if you're looking for a how-to manual. Instead, it's an engrossing and epic true story that at once puts you at ease and challenges you to live more freely. It's unlike any Christian book I've ever read. It was so crazy good that I got to the end and wished there were more."

—HAYLEY MORGAN, writer of thetinytwig.com

"I am a Susie Davis fan! Susie speaks to my soul. She draws me from the shore of safety into the deeper waters of the Spirit. *Unafraid* will beckon you to begin with abandon a new journey with God. Susie's soul is the inkwell, her heart is the quill, and her words are the invitation: fear not for the Lord is with you."

—RANDY PHILLIPS, lead pastor at LifeAustin Church and member of Phillips, Craig, and Dean

"When we bow to the god of fear, we think we will be safe, but that's a lie. Our lives diminish as fear gains more ground. Having witnessed her beloved teacher's murder, Susie Davis understands that bad things happen. That's what makes her journey from paralyzing fear to trusting faith so compelling. I can't wait to give *Unafraid* to some of my clients."

—LESLIE VERNICK, licensed counselor, relationship coach, speaker, and author of *The Emotionally Destructive Marriage*

"Susie Davis offers a timely message of hope in a world that seems completely out of control. This book is a very personal and honest account of her experience with trauma and subsequent fears. She offers profound lessons of faith and trust based on her extraordinary story. It is truly an amazing God-story of redemption and hope."

—DR. SAM ADAMS, psychologist and coauthor of *Out of Control: Finding Peace for the Physically Exhausted and Spiritually Strung Out*

"I've witnessed firsthand Susie Davis's incredible journey as she's learned to trust God in an unsafe world. *Unafraid* is the book Susie was born to write. Fears will be confronted. Chains will be broken. And multitudes of women will be set free to live their lives unafraid."

—VICKI COURTNEY, author of *Move On*

UNAFRAID

UNAFRAID

Trusting God in an Unsafe World

Susie Davis

WATERBROOK
PRESS

UNAFRAID
PUBLISHED BY WATERBROOK PRESS
12265 Oracle Boulevard, Suite 200
Colorado Springs, Colorado 80921

Details in some anecdotes and stories have been changed to protect the identities of the persons involved.

Trade Paperback ISBN 978-1-60142-639-0
eBook ISBN 978-1-60142-640-6

Cover design by Mark D. Ford

Published in association with the literary agency of The Fedd Agency Inc., P.O. Box 341973, Austin, TX 78734.

Published in the United States by WaterBrook Multnomah, an imprint of the Crown Publishing Group, a division of Penguin Random House LLC, New York.

WATERBROOK and its deer colophon are registered trademarks of Penguin Random House LLC.

Library of Congress Cataloging-in-Publication Data
Davis, Susie, 1963-
    Unafraid : trusting God in an unsafe world / Susie Davis. — First Edition.
        pages cm
    ISBN 978-1-60142-639-0 — ISBN 978-1-60142-640-6 (electronic) 1. Fear—Religious aspects—Christianity. 2. Trust in God—Christianity. I. Title.
    BV4908.5.D37 2015
    248.4—dc23
                                            2014041572

5660 9737

5/15

Printed in the United States of America
2015—First Edition

10 9 8 7 6 5 4 3 2 1

SPECIAL SALES
Most WaterBrook Multnomah books are available at special quantity discounts when purchased in bulk by corporations, organizations, and special-interest groups. Custom imprinting or excerpting can also be done to fit special needs. For information, please e-mail SpecialMarkets@WaterBrookMultnomah.com or call 1-800-603-7051.

For my dad

Because trees really are the best preachers

Contents

Introduction

The Invitation

At twelve years old I met Jesus. I adored him . . . everything about him. When I read the Bible and it said God had good plans for me, I believed every word.[1]

Then at fourteen I saw my teacher murdered. It was May, the end of junior high school, when a fellow classmate—a neighbor boy—walked into our classroom with a rifle and shot and killed my teacher.

God may have saved me, but the experience of witnessing a murder crashed in unexpectedly and made me afraid. So afraid that I felt as if I had lost God somehow—or, even worse, that he had lost me. At fourteen I was forced to try to come to terms with this big, bad world we live in, and I was very fearful.

I loved God, but I did not trust him. Trusting God meant things might go wrong again, and I couldn't afford to let that happen because then I would feel all the pain again. The pain of bad things. And with the pain, the lingering question, *why do bad things happen?*

I spent half my life being afraid, and by that I mean scared to stay alone in my house at night. As a teenager, I was so freaked out by being alone I would hide under the kitchen counter with the phone on my ear, anxious about things in the dark and terrified by the neighbor boy still living up the street.

The weird thing about being afraid for a long time is that you get comfortable with it. And before long you start to believe fear itself keeps you safe and keeps bad things from happening. I felt like fear protected me. As long as I stayed vigilant, cautious, and wary, nothing bad would happen. Instead of depending on God for protection, I held tight to something destructive. Like an addict, I depended on something harmful and dangerous. Something that became a tool for the Enemy to push me in the corner, keep me under the counter, beat me down.

I believed in fear.

I felt hopeless trying to live with a Savior who didn't seem to keep me safe from the bad things and was completely worn-out trying to take care of myself. Over the years my fears spiraled out of control. I was afraid for my children. I became the mom who hypermanaged, helicopter-parented, and over-thought every little thing, because fear told me that was my job. I obsessed about my husband's safety because fear lived by my side, whispering horrible things about the worst-case scenarios. If you had looked into my life, you would have seen me peeking in the closets for bad guys, double- and triple-checking doors at night, obsessively washing my toddlers' hands.

Fear infects your life in weird ways when you believe in it, always think on it, worship it. You become a fear-er. Only I didn't think I was a fear-er. I thought I was c-a-r-e-f-u-l. I thought I was being a good mom. A caring wife. But really, I was afraid. I couldn't see how fear changed me—and how the Enemy took advantage of me.

"Here begins the Good News about Jesus . . ."[2]

But God was not content to let me sit scared to death, scrunched under the counter, cowering, while the Enemy pounded me with more and more fear. Eventually I let God rescue me.

And he wants to rescue you too. I promise. God does not want you stuck under the counter or wherever the Enemy has you holed up. God wants you free. Really free. And he wants you with him . . . looking to him, trusting him, finding security in him.

By reading about how God has cared for me in some hard situations, I hope you will see how creatively and tenderly he cares for you. I pray you can learn to live unafraid in the midst of an often terrible and terrifying world because you know and believe in a real way that God has good plans for your life. And because, deep down, you are able to trust God. I pray you are able to know he loves you too much to ever abandon you in any situation. Not then, not now, not ever.

This is the invitation.

1

On the Curb

I don't actually remember my dad planting the cottonwood tree, but I know he planted it as a seedling. He always planted seedlings. I can picture him now, loading buckets of water into his red Volkswagen convertible. Like a big weeping willow sweeping back and forth in the wind, he moved from the hose by our house to his car, carrying the buckets. All this so he could water a little tree at the junior high school down the street. I was maybe six years old.

I remember he would put the pails on the floorboard of his old VW bug, and then he'd have me sit in the backseat between them so I could try to hold them still while he slowly drove the three blocks to the school grounds. Everything looked crazy out of control in those buckets. Water sloshed over the edges, soaking my T-shirt and shorts. Water rolled around on the floorboard. All this for a tree—a scraggly cottonwood he planted without permission on school property.

This particular cottonwood needed extra attention because there were no hoses nearby. After all, this tree wasn't supposed to be there. It wasn't a part of the master plan—at least not part of the school's master plan. That's why my dad had me help him water it.

My dad was a hip tree hugger before anyone knew what it meant to be green. As a matter of fact, if you look in his backyard today, you'll see five or six mismatched tubs full of dirt and little saplings. Cottonwoods, bur oaks, mimosas—my dad loves them all. He keeps them close to the house and waters them religiously with a nearby hose.

Eventually I inherited my dad's love of trees, but my reason is a little different from his. It's because I finally realized that God has been leaving me love notes all my life—and I don't mean scribbles on little pieces of paper. God has been leaving me tangible signs of how much he loves me. And most often God leaves me love notes through trees.

My dad always says trees are the best preachers, and I agree. Trees are the conduits for some of the biggest messages God has ever spoken to me. At every season in my life, there is a tree with

God saying, *I love you. I'm thinking of you. I'm protecting you. I have good plans.*

The curious thing is, my dad made me water the very tree that became one of the biggest love notes God ever wrote me. I just didn't see it at the time—or for a very long time, really.

It works like that sometimes. We don't see how God loves and cares for us, especially when we're afraid, and we mistake our lack of vision for a lack of God's care. Like a seed in the ground, God's care lies deep underneath, but sometimes we miss it.

THE GOD WHO SEES ME

At times in my life, I wish I were more like Hagar in the Bible. Here was a woman who experienced the reality of an unsafe world at the hands of someone who was supposed to take care of her. Pregnant and alone, she fled into the desert because she was terrified for her life. But God was right there. He was thinking of her, protecting her, and making good plans for her even when things looked bleak. Through an angel he comforted her with words of hope, promising that her baby would be safe. And there she confessed, "You are the God who sees me . . . who looks after me."[1]

God doesn't often speak through angels—at least not to

me. But he was speaking to me in other ways. I just had to pay attention.

God is speaking to you too. It may not be through an angel or through trees, but he is speaking. Directly to you.

There are so many times in normal, everyday life when it doesn't really seem as if God is doing anything special—aside from keeping the sun up in the sky and other such wonders. But the little things? Do you ever feel that he is too busy to be in the smallest details of life? I did.

But the Bible says God pours down his blessings.[2] *Pours down his blessings.* Like big, sloshing buckets of water being poured over a tiny cottonwood tree. Now I see that's me getting soaking wet with all those blessings. But it took me years to recognize it, and I certainly didn't see it when I was fourteen. Then, and for a very long time, I felt cheated. And alone. I was completely hung up on the world being a big, bad place. I felt overwhelmed trying to take care of myself and understand everything.

Don't get me wrong. I prayed and held on to God as best I could. But I just didn't see the buckets of blessings. I didn't see God working. I got God as the creator of the universe, the sustainer of the world. But I just wasn't so sure he was into the little stuff—like watching after me in my everyday life.

Now I know God always wants my attention. I have found he'll stop at nothing to get it. But it's hard to see God's love and care when fear is staring you in the face. Fear makes you blind . . . and deaf and dumb. Unable to see or hear or feel those buckets of favor pouring over you. Unable to utter thanks for all the tiny drops of God's goodness.

CURB TO CURB

I'm still trying to figure out exactly when and how fear first entered my life, because I don't remember being afraid as a young child. I do remember boldly running over to my neighbor Frances's house when I was five because she had a gum drawer, and when I was seven, I fearlessly rode my bike too fast down the hill on our street and busted my chin. I also remember at the age of nine playing kick the can with the neighbor kids in the cove at dusk all summer long.

I grew up in the kind of neighborhood where you could play outside long past dark, and there was no reason to be afraid. That was a time when kids could run yard to yard, house to house, and at the end of the day moms would yell out the front door for their kids to come home for dinner. My home, our street, our little cove community felt safe.

My best friend, Julia, lived right across the street from me. I loved going to Julia's. Her mom, Anna, used to make us snacks of chocolate ice cream and salty skinny pretzel sticks. When I was very young, I wasn't allowed to go to Julia's without

9

permission or to cross the street by myself. If Julia and I couldn't get our moms to agree to a play date, we'd sit on the curbs in front of our houses—Julia on one side of the street and me on the other—and we would talk there. When cars started down the street, we would scoot back into our yards, because our mamas told us cars were dangerous. But curb to curb, life was safe.

Wouldn't it be great if we could rewind to another time or do life curb to curb and make it safe? Then we'd never have to be afraid. We'd never have to worry about our babies getting sick. We'd never have to watch news stories about people being gunned down in shopping malls or school-yards or churches. Never worry about abductions or all the other monstrosities wrecking people's lives. Never worry about divorce or losing a job or making ends meet. Never worry about those things that make you worry. If we could only live unafraid.

But life is not a simple math equation. One plus one rarely equals two. So we worry and feel afraid. Have you noticed how fear doesn't follow any rules? Fear is a rule breaker. A fake-out. A liar. And we all learn to fear soon enough. Even if you haven't had bad things happen directly to you, I'll bet you learned fear anyway. Fear creeps in through books, television, and other people's stories.

I think I first learned fear that way. So much so that by the time I was ten and in fourth grade, I didn't want to stay home alone. My mom was a teacher, so she wasn't home in the afternoons. I let myself in the house through a door that was left unlocked or with a key hidden in the garage. Pretty standard for the seventies.

Sometimes, after I'd let myself into the house after school, I'd hide in the closets. Squished in between the coats in the hall closet, I felt safe. But then it would get quiet. And I'd listen . . . for fear . . . never realizing it was sitting right next to me.

Some days I would peptalk myself into being brave. I'd march into the house, turn on the television, and watch *Little House on the Prairie* so loud that I couldn't hear the fear. I needed the goodness of the show to drown out the bad stuff in my mind. *What if there's someone in the house with me? What if that creaking is someone walking around upstairs? What if our little sheltie can't fight off the bad guys?* I was a ten-year-old kid with a big imagination.

My friend Cat and I now tease each other because we know we're HSP (highly sensitive people). We're the first to hear a baby crying on an airplane or notice that the drummer's too loud on stage at church. We get extra cold if the air conditioner is blowing hard, and we're likely to say so. Who knows? Maybe being an HSP or having a big imagination was why I was so aware of the voice of fear at a young age. But I also think the Enemy wants a foothold anywhere he can find one. For me, the foothold was fear.

Katie, a young mom I mentor, told me that when she was little, she used to fall asleep listening to talk radio. She said she needed the friendly voices when she fell asleep because there were so many angry voices in her family, and they made her feel afraid. Fear started calling her name as a child.

And my friend Ronne told me that when she was young, after her mom tucked her into bed at night, she would crawl on the floor to her mother's bedroom. She was afraid of the shadows standing behind her bedroom window because once she had seen a man staring in at her. She worried he'd come back one day and steal her away.

Fear whispers when we're young. It follows us when we're older. And somewhere along the way, we start to think it's normal to be afraid.

Have you ever experienced this? Letting the what-ifs overwhelm you? Turning up the *Little House* volume loud so you can't hear the questions in your head: *What if something happens to my kids at school? What if my husband doesn't make it home from his business trip? What if God gives me more than I can handle?*

No matter if we're ten or thirty or fifty, I think we're all little on the inside when it comes to fear. We're always looking for safety. For places where nothing bad ever happens. But the quest for safety and insulation from anything bad takes us to all the wrong places instead of to the right one.

THE ANTIDOTE TO FEAR

At twelve I thought I had met the antidote to fear: Jesus. My family was at a Young Life retreat, and a college kid named Kenny took time to sit down and tell me the story of Jesus and how he had changed his life. I had heard about Jesus before in church services, but the Jesus I learned about in church didn't seem as real to me as the Jesus that Kenny described.

Kenny and I sat at the edge of the Frio River while upstream kids played guitars and sang. It was kind of romantic, and Kenny was kind of cute. But at some point I stopped caring about how cute Kenny was and started listening to his story. I was overwhelmed at what he told me—that God loved me so much he sent Jesus to rescue me from all sin.

I didn't feel as though I had a lot of sin, but I knew I had enough to need Jesus. I knew I needed relief from the thick, heavy, bad feelings I got when I messed up. Like how I felt when I was mad at my friends but lied by saying no when they asked if I was mad. Or when I was rude to my mom for dumb things like how she ironed my shirt. Or when I cheated in math class by peeking at my neighbor's work sheet, or when I said mean things about people I didn't like at school. Stuff that might not seem big to an adult but is grave for a sixth grader.

So I prayed right there, with big tears streaming down my face, for God to be my everything. For Jesus to be my hero, to take away all the blah, yucky stuff clogging up my heart. And Jesus said yes to me.

Back at home I started reading the Bible, and it was even better than I thought. When I read my Living Bible, Jesus was all rainbows and butterflies. He was all good news, good plans, and a good life. The Young Life kids who loved Jesus in such a real way were now streaming in and out of our house because my parents offered to host weekly dinners for them. They were so happy and funny and free. I was all in with this Jesus. I felt nothing could come between us.

But, of course, something did. Something horrible crashed in unexpectedly. And along with it a stronghold of fear that lasted more than a decade and crippled my ability to see how God flooded my life with love. For so long I was blind to his love notes.

2

Promises

Every once in a while, you meet a person who blows promises all over your life like a dandelion wish in springtime. This person speaks over you, telling you things about your character or your talent or your future that you never would have seen or believed otherwise.

Kenny was the person who spoke the promise of Jesus into my life. He was the one who took the time to explain how much God loved me. Kenny helped twelve-year-old me see God was not pointing a finger at me for the things I felt bad about; rather, he was waiting with arms outstretched.[1] This is the best promise I've ever embraced.

Just a few years later, when I was fourteen, I received another promise. It was from my eighth-grade English teacher, Mr. Grayson. He was the person who spoke the promise of writing into my life. It wasn't some grandiose revelation but a quiet affirmation over his desk after school one day. I was turning in a revision on an essay that we had gone back and forth on. I was tiring of the process, and Mr. Grayson knew it. As I handed him the paper, he asked me to sit down for a minute. I pulled up a chair, facing him across his desk.

"Susie, I know you're tired of rewriting this paper, but you need to know something. You're a good writer. A really good writer. I think you could do something pretty important with this gift of yours, and that's why I'm requiring so much work from you. I see it right here on the page. You have a gift."

Mr. Grayson's words were a promise. One I would think about for a very long time. A promise, like the Jesus promise, that has permeated every single area of my life.

BAD STUFF HAPPENS

I don't remember seeing my dad's cottonwood tree when I walked into Murchison Junior High School and into Mr. Grayson's class that May morning in 1978. But I must have walked right by it. And I know it was way more than the scraggly little Charlie Brown tree I had watered with my dad when I was six years old.

Since cottonwoods grow as much as five feet a year, my dad's tree was easily thirty to forty feet tall with a large, leafy canopy of shimmering heart-shaped leaves. Pretty hard to miss. But I'm sure I missed it the morning of the murder. And I didn't think about its significance—how my dad and I planted it together—or understand it was a love note from God until I was in my late twenties.

The Bible says we cannot understand the activity of God.[2] I couldn't agree more wholeheartedly. We can't begin to understand how God thinks of us and loves on us in the most intimate ways. So sweet and so tender, like an anxious young lover leaving vulnerable little notes scattered all over the place.

God's thoughtfulness is easy to miss when you look around the world and see all the horrible stuff going on. Because you realize God could stop a lot of the bad stuff, and he doesn't always.

I was in the eighth grade when the bad stuff crashed into my life. It was the end of the school year, and I was nearly free of junior high. It was a humid spring morning, typical Austin weather.

There were twenty-eight of us sitting in the classroom, which was on the first floor by a side exit door. Our teacher, my creative encourager, Mr. Grayson, sat perched on a stool in the front of the room. He was getting onto us for being rowdy the day before when we had a substitute, but his warm tone and smiling eyes contradicted his words. We knew he wasn't mad; it wasn't his nature. And I know he wasn't surprised at our rowdiness. He was used to dealing with our energy and antics. In fact, I think he appreciated that about us because it reflected our zeal for learning from his inspired teaching.

Noticing that one of our classmates, John, wasn't in the room, Mr. Grayson asked if anyone knew where he was. A moment later someone pointed at the window and said, "There's John right there." And sure enough, he walked right by the classroom window on his way toward the side door leading into the building.

Within seconds John walked into the room carrying a .22 rifle. He stood squarely in front of Mr. Grayson. John mumbled something, but with everyone talking I couldn't hear what he said. Then John calmly raised the gun waist high.

The scene in front of me wasn't making any sense in my brain. This was John. Quiet, shy John. My neighbor three doors up the block. The one I played kick the can with in the cove on warm summer nights and the boy I had known since elementary school. The one who always made good grades and never caused a problem. Here was one of the nicest kids in our class . . . holding a gun in front of my teacher? What was he doing?

We all sat there stunned. And for a second or two, I

wondered if it was some imaginative, preplanned lesson Mr. Grayson had dreamed up and John was in on. Or maybe John had brought the gun as a prop for his drama class. Because, strangely, here he was—a sandy-haired, shy thirteen-year-old holding a rifle ten feet from our teacher.

What happened next is a blur. Shock has a way of erasing details. But I do remember watching, stunned, as John fired the gun three times directly at Mr. Grayson. Three quick shots that sounded like a giant slamming a two-by-four against a concrete wall. Mr. Grayson fell hard to the floor. Out of the corner of my eye, I saw John turn around and walk out of the classroom as calmly as he had entered minutes before, leaving us there to deal with the gruesome scene.

Another split second of disbelief suspended all of us. We looked at each other in wide-eyed shock. Then the screaming started. Chairs overturned as we lurched from our seats. We were all scrambling to escape this temporary hell created by a boy, a gun, and a moment of pure madness. I looked at Mr. Grayson. Blood was spilling out of his ear. His face was quiet. His body was fighting for life.

Oh, dear God . . . please no. Please no.

We all ran out of the room, leaving Mr. Grayson alone. We scattered in different directions. Screams shattered the court-yard's silence. One of the students in my classroom ran all the way home. I wish I had run home too, but my friend Cheryle and I ran to the main office. Mrs. Fleury, the counselor, held us as we frantically told her John had shot Mr. Grayson.

Everything was tremendously chaotic. Deathly strange. There was no protocol for anything like this in the seventies. No handbooks on school violence and school safety. There was literally no plan in place at all.

From my location in the school office, I could hear everything in bits and pieces: the sirens and the story of how a coach caught John throwing his rifle in the bike racks and trying to run away. I heard how John's dad and brother had showed up in the principal's office, where they were holding John. That was only a few doors away from where Cheryle and I were holed up.

In the next hour the school staff gathered us in the choir room and then lined us up to go outside. I dutifully followed the adults in charge and could see they were loading us onto a yellow school bus. As I rounded the corner to step inside the bus, I was horrified to see news reporters swarming around us like flies on road kill. I felt so angry I wanted to hit somebody. While we were mourning, they were gawking.

I got on the bus and found a seat. I wasn't sure where we were going. We cried and talked, trying to make sense of why John shot Mr. Grayson. We sang hymns even though this was no Christian group. We were public school kids, frantically searching for any stability. Someone stood in the center aisle of the school bus and prayed for Mr. Grayson. And for John.

The bus rolled to a stop at the police station. Then they walked us into a big room with a sign on the door that read Homicide. I didn't know what that meant. Inside, there were seven or eight employees sitting at desks with typewriters. We waited and took turns as they recorded our individual stories, as if we each had something different to say. As if we could answer the whys.

By that time our parents were gathered in a room nearby, even though we weren't allowed to see them until every student finished giving details. More than three hours had passed since John walked into our classroom and blew up everything I knew of my life. Knowing my parents were that close but not being able to see them was like bleeding on an operating table, just waiting for the doctor to show up.

When the doors were finally opened, I collapsed into the safety of my dad's arms. Pressing my face into his lapel, I could smell home and comfort. The way things smelled when my mom was making dinner and my dad would walk in and put his briefcase and the daily paper on the old stereo by the back door. I was starving for comfort, but at that minute home felt far away. So far away I didn't know if I'd ever get it back.

My mom hugged me, crying. She was the one who got the call from the school after the shooting. She answered the phone, dressed only in a towel, dripping wet from a shower. All they said to her was, "Your daughter is on her way to the police station. If you would like to be with her, you need to go right now."

She had no idea what had happened. They wouldn't tell her, just as they didn't tell any other moms answering the phone that day. Again, no protocol in the seventies.

I left the police station with my parents. My dad shielded me from the curious onlookers, because by now the story was leaking out about how a kid shot his teacher at school in front of a room full of students.

As we were driving home, I kept thinking about John—how I felt as though I knew him but really didn't. And I kept thinking about Mr. Grayson—how I wished I had told him how much I appreciated him, how I loved his teaching, and how tightly I held on to the promise he spoke into my life about writing. Suddenly a realization hit me. "Mom, if Mr. Grayson dies . . . that will mean John murdered him."

"Oh, Susie . . . I thought they already told you . . ."

Wait. What? Mr. Grayson was dead? John murdered our teacher?

I started crying again, so hard I could barely breathe. I gripped the dashboard, shaking my head back and forth while screaming, "No! No! *Noooooo!*"

Then I grabbed the handle of the car door, wanting to throw myself out while my mom was driving sixty miles an hour down the highway. I literally wanted to die that day. It was just too much.

I didn't realize it then, but that was the beginning of my breakup with God. I don't think I ever stopped loving him, but I definitely stopped trusting him. Because I knew he was big enough to stop the bad thing from happening—the whole big, bad thing. The incident that left a classroom full of kids absolutely traumatized and bewildered. The one that left a young bride a widow and a small child fatherless. The thing that left a kind and prominent Austin family wondering what had snapped in their thirteen-year-old son. God could have stopped it all. But he didn't.

IS GOD BREAKING A THOUSAND TINY PROMISES?

I'm wondering, what are the things in your life God could have stopped . . . but didn't? What was it that spun out of control to create the fears in your life? Was it personal? Did you experience something hard or painful? Or did something happen to someone close to you? Maybe your dad got cancer and died when you were twenty-five. Or your sister was raped in college. Or maybe it's not personal at all. Maybe you can't help but watch the news from around the world, and your heart breaks for all the horrible things people have to endure.

Yes, I feel it too—the broken world caving in on us. And sometimes, if I'm honest, it feels as if God is breaking a thousand tiny promises. There is just too much going on in our lives that doesn't seem like "plans for good and not for disaster."[3] It feels as if God turns his head away for a millisecond . . . and someone's world falls apart. Sometimes mine. I bet sometimes yours too. And that's scary. It feels as though God somehow abandoned us.

I felt abandoned that May day in 1978. Like God turned his head and my world crushed into pieces. I still loved God after the murder. I really did, but I didn't feel like I could trust him.

I felt about God the way my friend Karen feels about her husband. Married ten years with two children, she discovered he had been unfaithful to her in their marriage. Upon discovery of his infidelity, she questioned whether she would ever trust him again. Although he was a good father and an excellent breadwinner, he was an unfaithful husband. There was a lot good, but there was this one big, bad thing. Should she choose to stay in a hard relationship or just leave?

I saw God as a wrecked man because I felt as if he broke his promise to keep bad stuff from crashing in on my life. Though I'd decided at twelve I wanted Jesus to be my hero, he wasn't exactly the hero I'd hoped for. My kind of hero wouldn't let bad things happen to me. He would love me too much to put me through that kind of hell.

While I never thought about bailing on my faith, I certainly didn't believe I could count on God to take care of me. So along with the tragedy of the murder—and all the pain associated with that—I also felt the ache of abandonment. I felt twice cursed. The world is evil and God won't take control. Not even for me. This realization terrified me, and it carried with it hard questions.

Why God? Why?

Why turn your eyes away while the world breaks apart?

Why would you abandon me?

Why?

WHEN "WHY" OVERWHELMS

I don't know where your whys originate. Jim's wife was unfaithful to him. Bethany suffered familial sexual abuse as a child. Ann's dad abandoned her family. Scott endured a lengthy court battle over his work. My friend Christie got cancer right after her husband left her.

There are all kinds of things producing pain in our lives. And at some point in the process, we ask why, why, *why*?

Whys may even start as small seeds of hopelessness when we're tired, weak, or discouraged. When we compare, feel insecure, and question if God hears. When we wonder why we're not getting something we deserve.

The little why question is a cry, really. A deep-down,

guttural question leaking out of a vulnerable, aching heart. It's not a bad or wrong question, this why. David asked why all over Psalms. Jesus even asked why.[4]

When you hurt—when the circumstances are unbearable—the hard questions surface. There is nothing wrong with hard questions. The why question is not the problem. The problem is where it leads you. When sitting in the sad place of grief or the uncomfortable place of anxiety becomes too much, sometimes we find it easy to wander.

We adopt unhealthy behaviors in an effort to soothe the pain, to alleviate the fears. We drink to lose control and numb out, hoping to escape reality. Or we helicopter-parent to gain control, because we don't trust that God will really take care of our kids.

Or we desire knowledge to understand the circumstances and hit the inherent conflict of why head-on by engaging in conversations. We want answers, so we ask our friends. We read dozens of books thinking maybe the next one will finally explain it. Or we watch the news networks and listen for someone to answer this problem of fear and pain. And what happens is we get directed away from God. We hear these questions:

- Why would a loving God allow tens of thousands of people to be swept away in a tsunami?
- How could God allow a man to walk into an

elementary school and gun down a classroom full
of kindergarteners?

- What kind of God lets some guy fly an airplane
  into a building full of innocent people?

We look into our own lives and ask questions too:

- Why won't God let me have a baby?
- How could God let my family be destroyed by
  infidelity?
- Why won't God stop my child from being bullied?
- How come God didn't save my mom from dying
  of cancer?
- Why is God giving me more than I can handle?

It's the shift from grief to reasoning, from sadness to anger.
Instead of speaking to God, we speak about him. We question
his care, his love, his motives. We think, *He's holding out on us.
He hasn't protected us. He has exposed us to awfulness.*

Then we wonder, *What kind of God does that?*

UNFULFILLED EXPECTATIONS

Until the age of fourteen, I had an expectation of God. I
thought if Jesus was my hero, he would shield me from all the

bad things. Or that, at the least, bad things wouldn't impact me the same way they did people who didn't love God.

At a very young age, I saw God all wrong.

Being a Christian doesn't mean bad things won't happen. Bad, sad, horrible things will happen regardless of whether you're a Christian or not. And bad, sad, horrible things will hurt with equal intensity. Being a Christian does not safeguard you from a world of hurt. Jesus himself promises trials and sorrows.[5] And Jesus himself hurt.

So the big question is, *what then is the value of having a relationship with God?* If we're all going to get hit with the same awfulness, all feel the same dark pain, why be in a relationship with God at all?

I guess the answer would be, *so you can be in a relationship with God.*

We're all so interested in how things affect us that many times we miss the main thing: God. The Creator of the universe. The Creator of you and me.

He loves us. He wants us. He will stop at nothing to get us.

The problem is, we let the bigness of grief and pain overwhelm the obvious: God loves.

I hate this about myself, but sometimes I think I'm the center of my universe. I forget the whole idea of God as Maker and me as just me. I forget there's an actual structure in this seemingly chaotic life and God is at the tiptop of it. I forget to marvel in everyday amazement over the idea that God loves me.

God loves you too.

No matter where you are in your life and no matter where you are with God, he loves you. But he's also ridiculously protective of you. He's not content to let fear divide your heart in two and distract you from wholehearted affection.[6] God wants both our love and our trust. And he'll stop at nothing to get them.

3

The Losing Team

The summer following the murder I found myself restless for things lost because of the tragedy—namely, my childhood. So I climbed the huge live oak in our front yard and sat there on a low-lying limb, looking for the spot where my mom planted yellow daffodils Easters ago, letting my mind wander to a time when life didn't seem so complicated.

At nine years old I first learned to climb the big oak tree. Summer of '73. I'd hoist my foot in the old scar where the tree was pruned. Then I'd grab hold of the next higher branch and pull myself up until I was hidden in the branches. I'd sit there beneath the little emerald leaves, peeking at the enormous blue sky, letting the quiet sink in, feeling small but safe in the big, wide world.

Those were the summers of feet callused and blackened from running around barefoot through the neighborhood. Hot, sticky days cooled with purple Popsicles. Walking to the library to gather as many books as I could carry home in my arms. Sitting on the front porch at dusk until the soft Texas sun closed her eyes just so I could count all the fireflies dancing in the yard.

Those were the innocent years before I determined life should be managed and controlled to feel safe. Years before I had to fight to hold things together because I felt God allowed things to fall apart.

At some point after witnessing the murder, I came to understand my childhood was over that day in May. I also came to understand an even more difficult realization: *God's not all he claims to be. He held out on me, walked out on me, didn't care for me. And didn't stop the bad stuff from happening.*

Sure, God held the stars in place and managed the sun and moon, but on that terrible day in May, he was off doing bigger and more important things than caring about me. Though God spared my life the day of the murder, I lost the belief that he is good and kind and that he keeps us tucked safely by his side. So I allowed my heart to become divided, loving God but not trusting him. And I adopted a faith where I said and did the things I knew I should without negotiating the deep conflict sitting uncomfortably in my heart and mind.

I thought if perfect love drives out all fear,[1] I'd perfect my love for God by working harder at being sunshiny and positive. I'd go to church, memorize Scripture. I'd be a good Christian girl who knows that all things work out for the good for those who love the Lord.[2] I threw myself into the mechanics of Christianity because I desperately wanted to find the girl I was before the murder: the believer. The one who read the Bible and fell into God's promises easily. The one who was convinced of the goodness of God's character. I wanted to recover who I was before the bad thing happened. I wanted the life I lived before that day in May, the time when I wholly and simply trusted myself to God. But that girl seemed so far away. I wondered if she'd ever come back. It was as if all the goodness and innocence in my life had been blown away and, along with it, my trust in God.

READY TO GET AWAY

As I began my freshman year of high school, I didn't want to be different. I didn't want to be weak. And I definitely didn't want to be the sad girl forever tied to the tragedy of the murder at Murchison just four months earlier. So I walked away from all the confusing grief and the overwhelming darkness. I tried to quiet the questions, the conflicts, and the broken promises by distracting myself with life as usual: cheerleading, honor society, boyfriend, Bible study. But it didn't work. I now owned a kind of cut-and-paste theology with no depth of conviction. And I applied Scripture like Band-Aids over my shattered heart. I worked so hard that I broke apart even further on the inside. I spoke big words about loving and trusting God, but in reality I couldn't stay home alone, walk my neighborhood at dusk, or sleep in my room at night.

John scared me still because I wasn't exactly sure where he was after the murder. He never went to prison, and although I'd heard he was living with a family in Dallas, I worried that he still visited his parents' house, just three doors up from mine. Additionally, the motive for the murder was attributed to a diagnosis of schizophrenia. So I now had reason to fear something I couldn't easily identify: anybody with a condition I didn't understand.

At sixteen I experienced one of the scariest nights ever — the night of my first panic attack. My boyfriend walked me into my house, said good night, and walked out. Within five minutes of being alone, I freaked out and called my parents, begging them to come home, while I crouched under our bar counter. I sat there, terrified, quietly crying lest the imaginary monster upstairs hear and discover me. I thought I might die.

At seventeen I would drag my comforter into my parents'

room at night. Most nights I slept on the floor beside their bed. By eighteen I couldn't stay alone in my house even during the daytime. The big grandfather clock in the front hall, which used to be charming, turned creepy; the eerie hourly chime sounded like impending doom.

Although I loved Austin, I couldn't wait to graduate from high school and leave. Sometime between February and April of my senior year, I started to realize college wasn't just leaving home; it was an opportunity to start over. To escape. A chance to get away from the frightened, freaked-out girl I'd become.

The murder made a mental hoarder out of me, my mind stuffed with the grossest emotional baggage. Horrid memories stacked in mismatched boxes. What-if scenarios systematically organized, Rolodex style. My life from fourteen to nineteen was piled high, full of the trash that comes from a soul wounded from trauma.

But I was moving now, ready to leave behind the weak girl I'd become. At nineteen I was done being the girl who impulsively dragged her comforter down the hall to her parents' bedroom because she couldn't face her fears in the middle of the night. And I was embarrassed by her inability to stay home alone, exhausted by the mental gymnastics involved in simple things like backing the car down the driveway because worry asked whether to drive up the street past John's house or down the street past the school where the murder took place.

Finally it was all over.

Every monogrammed towel I packed signaled my fresh start. I was going to be different. Unafraid. My best self. My brave self. Hello, Waco, Texas. Hello, Baylor University.

It didn't occur to me that I had a sick heart. I thought Austin was sick. My neighborhood was scary. My house was haunted. And I made a simple, rational assumption: I was leaving all the baggage behind.

I cast all my hope on a new home. A new city. And a fresh start. Never realizing the demons would follow.

Setting Up House

Fear won't let the heart settle, even into happy places. Fear uproots the smallest hope and prevents new growth. And since I did nothing to face the issues inside, college couldn't fix me.

While I didn't wake up scared in the middle of the night and drag my comforter down the hall, it was only because I had two roommates sleeping in the same room with me. And about fifty new friends literally down the hall. Proximity to people I felt were safe made me feel safe.

But because my issue of abandonment by God ran deep and I had done nothing to sort out why God seemingly stands silent in the midst of bad things, I didn't get well. I loved God, but I didn't trust him.

I still read my Bible, journaled, and did my best to obey God, but I always entertained the need to take cover—just in case God disappeared again. Just in case he let me down. Working hard at being a good Christian girl did nothing to mend my mind.

The freshman year in college always feels jumbly, especially if you try to be someone you're not. My new, unfamiliar "best" self didn't fit. I desperately needed support—external structure for all the inside chaos—to hold up the carefully crafted facade. I wanted rules to make life manageable. Curbs to keep things straight.

So I chose diet rules. Make the food behave and gain control. Manage meals and get the desired outcome. Get command over something.

Every morning I carefully measured out cereal in a cup. Just 110 tiny calories. At lunch, though the cafeteria smelled warm, like meat and potatoes, I headed straight to the salad bar: lettuce greens, shredded carrots, and two tomato halves with no dressing. When hunger grew angry in my belly before dinner, I ignored it and subsisted instead on Diet Coke and bubble gum. When the scale scorned my weight, I would go days eating nothing but air-popped popcorn until the scale smiled again. Things felt right until I couldn't keep all the rules I'd created. An unscheduled cookie or a bag of french fries could throw me into a panic.

So I engaged in an on-again, off-again relationship with bulimia. But since bulimia didn't fit with my shiny best self, and it certainly wasn't a practice that could be kept secret in a dorm setting, I took a scary step. I told my parents. I thought maybe they could fix my issues.

I cried and explained that I had this huge food problem. That when things went wrong I made them right by throwing up. I don't remember all they said, but I do remember their sad, concerned faces. No doubt, it was a difficult situation for them. I cried, confessing the behavior I thought was the main problem. They offered what was the best advice at the time and what any parent would have said: stop throwing up.

When wounded people self-destruct, the most obvious solution seems to be to tell them to stop the behavior. Stop throwing up. Or stop drinking, raging, spending, cutting. Stop being afraid. Just stop it. But over the years we've all learned what's actually most helpful—and most painful—is to point to the dark hopelessness and see why the behavior started.

More than anything I wanted to stop the behavior. Clean it up. Make it right. But since I chose avoidance as a dance partner, the end of my deep fear issues was nowhere in sight.

I was nowhere near becoming unafraid. Nowhere near reconciling what I felt like was abandonment from God. Nowhere near comfortable with peace in Jesus instead of in my circumstances. So as much as I wanted to fix myself, I was really only begging for help in cleaning and reorganizing the mess my divided heart made of my life.

The strangest thing happened though: I did stop throwing up. But only because a nutrition professor at Baylor I confided in told me two very important things. First, she told me I was wrecking my body for my future children. I hadn't considered that, and I wanted healthy babies. But second, and probably more compelling, she told me I needed counseling to get to the root of much deeper emotional problems.

I left her office and never threw up again because the idea of hurting my unborn children scared me, but the idea of uncovering "deeper emotional problems" terrified me. If throwing up meant something was really wrong with me, I figured I'd just quit. Because I thought counseling was for people like John with deep, dark problems. The kind of people who walk into a room and blow the world to pieces, not people like me who just need a little help not eating too many cookies. And frankly, counseling didn't fit my good-girl Christian image any more than bulimia did. So I quit throwing up.

Oh, what a mess. I was just sweeping symptoms around, never realizing I made room for seven other spirits more wicked.[3]

I thought I was gaining control and mastering my habits, but my insistence on neglecting the essence of my issues with God only set me up for more problems later on.

A TEAM PLAYER

Behavior is never the main issue. Belief is.

Jesus asks, "Why are you afraid?"

He is not poking around, trying to get us to change the way we act. Or be a better self. He is getting at how we believe.

Jesus asks, "Do you still not have faith in me?"[4]

Now I realize honesty would have been far better than sweeping things around. I wish I'd tried that with my younger self. But I didn't.

If I had honestly faced Jesus's questions in my Baylor days, I would have answered with this:

- I am afraid you are not really in control.
- I am afraid you stand beside tragedy but not in it.
- I am afraid your goodness is weak and the Enemy is stronger.
- I am afraid of something bad happening again.
- I am afraid because I love you but I do not have faith in your ability to care for me.

That is what I would have said. But instead, I tried to create systems for living with the monster called fear. I didn't like fear, but I felt fear was essential to feeling safe. Fear was necessary for survival. Fear was my savior because fear protected me.

Fear became as big as Jesus. Sometimes bigger. And many times way more real than Jesus. I had absolutely no idea how to live without fear. I couldn't be ugly and honest with Jesus. I couldn't negotiate the perceived loss.

Are you living with fear? Somehow believing fear keeps you safe? Safer than Jesus can?

Does fear insulate from rejection? Or protect from isolation? Does it keep your children secure? Safeguard them from bad decisions?

I mean, if you could honestly answer Jesus's questions— *Why are you afraid? Do you still not have faith in me?*—what would you say?

My friend Annie says she's afraid she's going to get sick and die from some horrible disease silently growing in her body even though there is absolutely no evidence she's sick at all. David says he's afraid there will be no provision for his family if he stops working hard, so he lets the unknowns of tomorrow fuel his fear-induced work ethic. Kate says she's afraid people won't include her if she doesn't wear the right clothes and live in the right neighborhood, so she endlessly dwells on how to secure the approval of her friends. Scott is sure his kids won't do well enough in school to get accepted to college if he stops hounding them, even though he recognizes the pressure he puts on them is wrecking the relationship.

It's fear. Whispering. Calling out to us. Bossing us around.

Keeping us busy. Much too busy to sit still long enough to answer honestly the questions Jesus asks of us.

THE LOSING QUARTERBACK

It's like the quarterback hero who throws an interception, losing the football game—and the championship—on national television. Well, so he's a great guy and you love him, but he lost the game. In front of everyone.

God lost the game. It's obvious. And God keeps losing the game to violence and tragedy. He loses to cancer. And adultery. Right?

So the question becomes how to cheer for the losing team. I figured the nicest thing to do was not draw a lot of attention to the losing quarterback, Jesus. Yes, he's there. We like him. Rah-rah. But over here on the sidelines, we work other plans. We collaborate with fear. Because fear is a better player, a smarter player.

When you strategize with fear, you have more control. There are plans to make and actions to take. Well, sure, it means you're teaming up with anxiety and worry—and, on occasion, bullies named hypochondria and paranoia—but it's so much better than blindly believing an undersized quarterback will win the game by faith. Right?

If you had told me I was picking the wrong side—playing

my life for the Enemy—I would have told you that you were crazy. I would have pointed to my love of God, my Christian activities, my spiritual devotion.

But all those Baylor years when I didn't want to be the wounded girl and I tried to live life as usual, I was picking the wrong side by believing fear and worry were the solutions to my problems. Life after the murder would never be usual. I carried around a deep wound, one aching out my insides. I thought facing the darkness meant I would always be sad. I did not want to face my Gethsemane, the place where Jesus cried out, "My Father, if it is possible, let this cup pass from Me; yet not as I will, but as You will."[5]

I had no idea God would do trades: joy for mourning, and praise for despair.[6]

I had no idea that in turning around to face God and fighting it out the way Jacob did in the Bible,[7] I would get a blessing.

So I sat with the subversive team, training for the worst.

Mainly I had an obsessive fear of violence. I was terrified I'd be a part of bad things happening again. It didn't help that Baylor would regularly highlight scary stories in an effort to keep young coeds safe. And it didn't help that bad things happened to some of my friends. My best friend was molested by a drunk; a sorority girl was raped by a fraternity guy.

Violence became a giant. Fearing was my safety. I was just

like the anxious Israelites. No Canaan for me. No "land flowing with milk and honey,"[8] because there was a giant in the way. Like the Israelites, I craved slavery. Yes, better to stay safe inside the torment of fear than to step out and face the giants.

As a fear-er, I felt it was better to eat certain foods, follow certain rules, and be around people who thought like I did rather than listen to the Calebs of the world telling me I could take the giants in the land.[9] Better to triple-check the doors, look in the closets, and warn the people I loved about the giants out there than to listen to God.

Better to be enslaved to the safety of fear—and seek to enslave others—than to risk stepping out and having something bad happen.

Fear-ers like me are forgetful. Just like the Israelites, we get from one season to the next, repeating the same lame attempt to protect ourselves, forgetting it is God who keeps the Enemy at bay. God who keeps our bodies whole. God who holds our children in his hand. God who wills protection, rest, and peace. The Enemy can do nothing to us without God's permission.[10]

Fear-ers are addicted to the delusion of safety. Evil doesn't enter only through unlocked doors. You can't avoid cancer just because you're careful. Seat belts don't save everybody, do they?

When we make even tiny little places for this thing called fear, we find ourselves apart from God. Apart from his mercy. Running so hard we're completely exhausted—"eating the bread of anxious toil"[11] —unsettled, upset, and jumbled. Because there is no peace.

THE SPIRIT OF FEAR

Back then I had no idea fear had a name, a presence, a persona. I actually thought fear was a helpful feeling. When your house is on fire, you are afraid, so fear helps you run out, and it saves your life. I thought all fear was like that fear.

But the kind of fear I packed up and carried with me to college was not that fear. Not a fleeting impulse that saves you from a burning house. It was dread. A kind of black-and-white horror infiltrating all the empty spaces in my head.

Dread is riding the brakes just in case. It's thinking ahead to what hasn't happened but might. It's the most terroristic of worries because it causes us to shrink back from faith. And it displeases God.[12]

You know that feeling you get when the landline wakes you up at one o'clock in the morning? You run for the phone, but no one is there. So you hang up the receiver slowly, standing there, shivering in your nightgown, waiting for it to ring again. When it doesn't, you walk slowly back to bed, crawl in, pull up the covers, and look for the moonlight through the curtains, listening.

That's when the dark thoughts start and fear creeps in. You

imagine all the things that might have happened to the people you love: accidents, car wrecks, heart attacks. Surely the bad news is there, sitting on the other side of the receiver. You're just waiting for the phone to ring.

PICKING SIDES

Author John Eldredge talks a lot about "making agreements" with the Enemy. He says that one of the tactics most often employed by Satan is a subtle, sometimes rational thought that is against God's truth.[13]

For me, there were plenty, but one of the most dangerous agreements I made was believing fear made me safer. That a big dose of caution was necessary for a good life, a safe life.

It starts innocently enough when we hear people's stories. The woman raped in the parking lot. The child abducted from the playground. The couple robbed at gunpoint in their own home. We hear these horrible stories every day on the news and sometimes in our own neighborhoods. They alarm us. They terrify us, right? But they also motivate us to be wary. To avoid the danger. Curtail mistakes.

And if we're completely honest, our initial empathy with someone else's horrible story is overrun by gross curiosity. We want the opportunity to practice personal caution at the victim's expense. We take notes on what to do or not to do to keep bad things from happening to us and the people we love.

All the note gathering is an opportunity for the Enemy to speak into our lives. And as we listen, we get an earful of subtle, rational thoughts that stand against the truth of God.

I felt that if God couldn't help me prepare for the worst, I would. Of course, getting an education from the Enemy about the world creates suspicion, desperation, and despair.

John Eldredge also said, "Demons smell our struggles like sharks smell blood in the water."[14]

I was struggling. And the sharks were circling.

But I made more agreements as the years went on. And the Enemy's influence in my life got stronger.

4

Easy Prey

I held tightly to my father's arm and steadied myself as the wedding coordinator adjusted the long train of my candlelight gown and then gently straightened my delicate veil. The moment had arrived. There was a hush as the doors opened. I glanced up at my dad, and he looked down at me, beaming. It was time. We slowly walked down the aisle, moving in rhythm to Pachelbel's Canon in D, smiling at the sweet friends and family gathered at my wedding. And then I caught Will's eyes and felt a rush of joy. We were finally here. I was marrying my high school sweetheart, the man of my dreams, a guy I knew would love, honor, cherish, and *protect* me.

"Who gives this woman to be married to this man?"

I moved my arm from my father's to my soon-to-be husband's. From one strong man to another. I felt safe.

After a delightful honeymoon in Maui, sunning on white sand beaches and drinking virgin piña coladas, we set up house in two cities, Austin and Fort Worth. At just twenty-four, Will pastored our first church in Austin while completing his master's degree in Fort Worth. And at just twenty-one, I managed two small apartments. Friday through Sunday we made our life in Austin, pastoring a start-up church planted by our home church. Monday through Thursday we made our life in Fort Worth as young seminarians. Life was busy, but we were young and determined.

I felt sure my fear issues would diminish because of the newfound security I had in sleeping next to my strong, confident husband, who promised he would protect me. But I didn't feel especially secure when he wasn't around. I remember many days climbing the concrete stairs to our little apartment in Fort Worth with grocery bags in hand, wondering if someone was hiding in my apartment. As I reached the entrance, I would place the bags at my feet, unlock the door, and then quickly swing it open wide. I'd hurriedly walk in, look in both closets and our walk-in pantry, and then lift the dust ruffle to glance under the bed. When I knew the apartment was safe, I'd go back and gather the groceries where I left them, then close and lock the door until Will came home for dinner, hours later. I kept up this routine, *just in case*.

And there were nights I'd lie next to Will and ask him to double-check whether he locked the apartment door, just in case. Or even look under the bed, just in case. Will desperately wanted to make me feel safe, so he did what I asked him even though he told me I had nothing to be afraid of. But for me, the only real assurance was checking the lock on the door and any hiding spaces, just in case. So fear tucked itself neatly into our new marriage.

LISTENING TO FEAR

All my bizarre behavior, panic attacks, and eventual neurotic parenting started by listening. I heard fear through the static, and I dialed in, listening to the whispers of worst-case scenarios.

Instead of listening to faith, which whispers truth about God's sovereignty and his absolute ability to take care of all things, I listened to fear, which whispers "what if" and "oh no" and "you better take care of yourself." *Just in case.*

Sure, it might seem normal I was scared after witnessing a murder and had some fear issues as a result. But a sixteen-year-old hiding under the counter and calling her parents to come home is not normal. And a twenty-one-year-old bride asking her husband to check under the bed is not healthy. Just as it's not normal for my forty-two-year-old friend, who is a mother of two children, to be unable to stay home alone with her kids overnight when her husband is out of town. And it's not healthy for my thirty-six-year-old friend to head to the emergency room several times a year because she assumes a bad headache is a sign of an aneurism. It's not normal to feel a sense of impending doom every time your kids leave for school in the morning. It's simply not healthy to make a place in your mind for even fleeting thoughts about ridiculously scary things that haven't happened. These are all signs that something is wrong, signals that help is needed.

The problem is, we are so used to everyone living in a paranoid, hypochondriac environment that we don't even see the problem. We are a people used to taking care of ourselves, grasping at control of whatever we can. A nation of "God helps those who help themselves." We eat whole foods. Avoid known carcinogens. Lock the doors. Turn on the alarms. Read the articles. Listen to the news. Gather in groups and talk about how to raise kids who will be safe, follow the rules, and avoid making bad choices. We're so consumed with trying to be careful that we don't realize the truth of the situation: Fear is our master. Fear whispers commands that we religiously obey, and then we reassure one another it's normal and necessary.

As safety seekers, we crave security. We want comfort and

a pain-free existence. So much of our energy is spent trying to avoid all the bad things. Being proactive about protection. Metaphorically checking the closets and peeking under the beds. It's energy spent planning for the worst. And while it might seem normal for where we live, it's not normal by heaven's standards.

I think that's why Jesus was always asking, "Why are you so afraid?"

He asked that question a lot, like in Matthew 8 where Jesus and his disciples were on a boat in a storm, and the disciples started freaking out. They woke up Jesus, screaming at him to help them because of the raging storm. In the middle of the turmoil—his voice rising above the frenzy—Jesus asked them, "Why are you so afraid? You have so little faith!"[1]

Let's be honest. Isn't that a little weird? That instead of immediately calming the storm, Jesus asked for trust? Instead of acknowledging the size of the storm and the disciples' need for security, he asked about their faith, and *then* he quieted the storm. Only after he addressed the obvious trust issue did he rebuke the waves. I think if ever there was a time for Jesus to tell the disciples to run for cover, it would have been in the middle of a stormy sea.

I am hard pressed to find any place in the Bible where Jesus told people to obey fear. I can't think of one story where he used fear as a motivation to induce behavior. No encouraging them to build big forts of protection around their own lives. Rather, he told them to trust him. To listen to his voice above the "what-if" and "oh no" and "you better take care of yourself." *Just in case.*

ESCAPE ROUTES

When people are exposed to the trauma of bad things or ongoing anxiety, they fight, flee, or freeze. I did all three. Plenty of all three.

But the bulk of what I did was flee. Run. Away. Far away. While I looked okay on the outside, there was this war going on inside my head. A constant onslaught of what-if voices. Fear in my face. And my conditioned response was to run.

I spent a decade in run mode. And it sits so deep inside me that it still pops up. Like last month. Will was coming in after being out of town, it was late, and I was coming home from an outdoor concert where our youngest was singing. I was driving up the big hill near my home, and I suddenly remembered something I deemed worrisome. Two weeks earlier I learned my husband left our house key on his key ring when he had his Jeep serviced. I call that a security breach. Will calls it a mistake. I asked, "Should we rekey the house?"

He asked, "How in the world would some employee at the Jeep dealership copy our key, stake out our house, and get in?"

Fear still speaks to me. Whispers violence. Tells me the worst thing could happen. Warns me to take care of myself.

As I was driving up the big hill near my home, suddenly I heard this in my head: *There is a man in your house. He is waiting for you. The worst is about to happen.*

And my immediate response was, *Maybe I should make a shopping run at Target and stay there until Will gets back so I don't have to enter the house alone.*

That's running. To Target, as if Target will protect me. Or the strangers at Target will. Huh?

Gratefully, I recognized this as an irrational fear. And there is a difference between a rational fear and an irrational fear. If the house is burning, get out. But if the house is only burning in your head, there's no need to run.

I didn't run to Target. Instead, I practiced something I wish my sixteen-year-old self had known—and even my twenty-one-year-old self. I stomped on the voice in my head by continuing to drive up the hill. Then I pulled into my driveway and got out of my car in the dark, put the key in the front door, and walked in. And I was scared, still feeling the physical effects of my thoughts, my emotions. The point here is, I didn't run away from home, because I replaced a lie with the truth: God's got me in the palm of his hand.[2]

I didn't wait for Will, making him the basis of my security as I would have in the early years of our marriage. Running to

Target and waiting for Will are escape routes. Places for me to seek security instead of trusting God.

RUNNING AWAY FROM HOME

The problem with fear is, it always leads us far away from God. Fear drives us into isolation, away from faith, away from peace, and away from security. While we imagine fear protects us, it actually leaves us more vulnerable. We listen intently to all fear is saying, and then we find ourselves under the counter crying. Or at Target.

We are running from God when we say we trust him, but we won't ever leave our babies with a caregiver. Running when we double- and triple-check the lock on the door. Running when we give our eight-year-olds cell phones so we can constantly text to keep tabs. Running when we let our work life dominate our schedules because we fear for tomorrow's provision. Running when we won't let our husbands leave on business trips or our kids go on mission trips because we're so worried for their safety.

What about you? Do you run to your husband for security? To your friends for reassurance? To social media for status? To your doctor for healing? To your job for provision? To the country club for prestige?

We're neurotic moms. Overbearing dads. Anxious wives and

weary husbands. We're men and women who know God stands strong and ready, but we run away instead of turning to him.

All my running scared didn't keep my kids safe. My oldest got lost on a mountain in Rocky Mountain National Park when he was only thirteen. My middle daughter got second- and third-degree burns on her body from boiling cooking oil. And at eight my youngest got thrown from a horse while going over a jump—right in front of me. My running didn't safeguard my husband from getting hit by a car while cycling.

My endless running and fearing never magically encircled my family in some sort of golden halo of safety. All my fear did was make me super tired. And it created distance between me and the people I love. My kids called their dad when they wrecked the car or got hurt—so they wouldn't stress Mom out.

That's what listening to the Enemy does to us. It divides and separates us from the God we want to trust. While I thought listening to fear made my family safe and secure—like chicks huddled under a mother hen—the Enemy was actually isolating me even further. With his slow, insidious whispers, he was pulling me away and then binding me up in anxiety. Winding me so tightly I was obviously not the person to call in an emergency. I was far too fragile, wrapped up in the weirdness of a fear-driven life.

All because I agreed with the demonic notion there must be a better way. A better life than the one God had planned for me.

While I was seeking strength and protection in control, I was actually just running away from home.

Because God is home.[3] He is our refuge, our strength. Our ever-present help. He is our comfort. And our peace.

But until we believe, we run, dripping wet with the sweat of worry. Distrusting God. Suspicious of his plans. Because that's what worry says. It says, "I don't trust God. I have a feeling God isn't looking out for me." The bottom line is, worry says God is a liar.

Worry is not a friend. It's not like inviting some cute, fuzzy kitten to curl up in the corner of your mind. Worry is a cat—but the bigger kind.

WHO IS STALKING YOU?

For more than a decade, I was easy prey for the Enemy. He only had to look my direction, and I'd run and duck under the counter. I'd hide inside all my safety rules. I'd hold a white-knuckled grip on the little bit of happiness I managed to squeeze out of my life. And I'd sit there waiting until I felt safe enough to crawl out. I was broken for so long, all because the Enemy learned my vulnerabilities very early.

He sniffs them out much like the lynx I saw on the front porch of our family cabin in Estes Park, Colorado, early this spring. I was sitting in the big bedroom downstairs, typing away, when I noticed two pointy ears peeking above the windowsill. A rush of adrenaline shot through me. I tiptoed to the window and spied a rare Canada lynx. I frantically grabbed for my cell phone, desperate to capture a picture and share it with my family. We've seen bears, badgers, foxes, coyotes, and even weasels at the cabin but never a lynx.

I watched the lynx through the window as it methodically sniffed each corner of the deck in front of me. Slowly and quietly he moved from one corner to the next. What in the world was he up to? Then finally he moved closer and closer to where the deck met the cabin wall, and suddenly I remembered—this was the spot I often saw a mama rabbit dart in and out.

Oh dear.

I heard a squeal. Then I watched as the lynx walked right in front of where I was standing, tucked behind the draperies. He had a baby bunny in his mouth. Little fuzzy legs dangling, wiggling frantically. The cat dropped down on all fours and ate the head first, then consumed the rest of the bunny's body. It was all over in less than three minutes. He licked the small drops of blood left on the ground, then got up and walked to the rabbit's nest again. I instinctively tapped on the window, my heart overwhelmed for the babies. I didn't want to see it again. The lynx looked up and stared in my direction for several seconds. Though this lynx was not a large cat, probably not much more than forty pounds, I was grateful for the thick window between us. He walked nonchalantly from the porch to the field in front of the house. Camouflaged by the tall mountain grasses, he was gone.

Watching the whole thing transpire, I couldn't help but feel God gave me a picture of what the Enemy does with us. He sniffs out our vulnerabilities. Patiently waits until he finds just the right spot. Then quietly goes in for the kill. When he has us in his grasp, he intends to kill us by devouring our trust in God. The lynx ate the head of the rabbit first. I think the Enemy starts there with us also. He makes a bid for our minds. Our little feet are dangling, wiggling in restless anxiety, and the Enemy whispers lies:

- God is not watching out for your children.
- God is not going to provide for your needs.
- God has lost control of the world.
- God is holding out on you.

It's when we agree with him in our minds—even in the smallest degrees—that the Enemy takes us whole. Just like the bunny, swallowed up in less than three minutes.

The Enemy stalks me, but by God's grace and the truth of Scripture planted deep in my mind, I am able to pry my head from his fierce grasp.

Like last winter when my husband decided to go camping

in Colorado . . . by himself . . . in January. Now, I have to be completely honest. A little part of me doesn't like it when Will does stuff like that. And I wonder why he can't just love golf. Something safer, tamer. But, no, Will loves hiking and mountains and adventure. I think sleeping in a tent on a mountain in the snow sounds really scary. And really cold. And dangerous.

Despite my fears Will went camping. And because he was camping remotely somewhere in Colorado, he was out of cell phone range. That evening I pulled on my coat to take a walk around the neighborhood, still missing him and thinking of him in those mountains all alone. I wasn't even a block from home when I imagined Will being stalked by a mountain lion. I could even picture the headline: "Texas man killed and eaten by mountain lion while camping in Colorado." The farther I walked, the more I filled in the details in my mind. It was dusk, and he would be sitting in his tent when the big cat pounced through the thin, orange lining, clawing at his body. There would be blood all over the snow. I imagined Will on that cold mountain trying to fight off the cat alone.

I got so caught up in this crazy, made-up scenario that I actually began to cry. One little tear after another streamed down my cheeks. I shot up a frantic prayer that if Will was attacked by some mountain creature, he would either get out alive or die quickly and not be in pain.

Then more images set in. First a mountain lion. No, maybe

a bear. Then a pack of wolves. All attacking my poor husband. As I pulled my coat sleeves down over my frozen fingers, I worried about how Will would escape these terrors.

More tears. More prayers.

And then I started getting mad, thinking about how impossibly selfish it was for Will to camp in the mountains in the winter with all those ravenous animals waiting to eat him. If he did survive, I thought about how I'd tell him a thing or two about camping in the mountains alone. About doing stuff that scares me. Dangerous stuff like being away from home and driving in snow and camping in the mountains and making me nervous and unsettled and teary and frightened and, and, and . . .

Suddenly it occurred to me. I was the one getting attacked . . . by fear. I was being stalked and taken down and eaten alive. Right there on the safe little street where I live. The Bible talks about it when it says, "Be self-controlled and alert. Your enemy the devil prowls around like a roaring lion looking for someone to devour."[4]

The Enemy knows just where to grab for me. Pouncing in with outrageous ideas and ridiculous scenarios, fear falling like new snow. The Enemy knows that when I listen to fear, it quickly leads to distrust.

Distrust in God. And his provision. And his plan.

We don't have the luxury of listening to the Enemy's lies if we desire to live free from fear and worry. And we don't have the option of letting lies settle into our minds if we intend to allow God his rightful place in our lives. So we must pray for discernment to recognize the Enemy's bid for our minds and then do something about it. Speak the truth:

- God is watching out for my children.
- God will provide for my needs.
- God has not lost control of the world.
- God is not holding out on me.

I know this: Will's safety is not dependent on his location. And neither is mine. The real threat is a wandering, vulnerable heart. A mind filled with lies, apart from God.

How God Gives Rest

It has taken me a long time to understand how the Enemy stalks me and how he seeks to take me down through fear. It's taken me years to recognize the Enemy sniffing around my life, looking for vulnerabilities. And though I do lean into and appreciate Will's role in my life as a provider and protector, I realize he is not my ultimate provider and protector. That's God's job. This truth has changed me.

As a matter of fact, if my fifty-year-old self could have

talked to my twenty-year-old self, my newly married self, and told her I'd see Will off for an out-of-town meeting in Nashville without freaking out, she would have said, *No way. That's totally crazy!* But that's exactly how I felt when Will left town recently, because all these years later God has mended my divided heart. Something my younger self didn't think was necessary or even recognize as a problem. While my younger self wouldn't even consider staying home alone for all the fear playing games in her head, now when Will is out of town, I recognize the Enemy will make a bid for my heart by replaying old tapes. But instead of following along, I grab my big Bible, open it to Psalm 3, and plop it down on the pillow next to mine. Then I say a prayer something like this:

> *God, be over this whole house. Inside it. Standing at*
> *every opening. This house is a house of peace. You give*
> *rest to your loved ones, even in their sleep.*[5] *Give me rest*
> *now.*

And then miraculously I fall to sleep. No listening for creepers. No lying there wondering if Will's okay, if all my kids are safe. Just off to sleep.

I put the Bible on Will's pillow next to me because it's like a sword. That's what it says about itself.[6]

The Bible is a weapon. Not a weapon to thump on an intruder but a weapon to fight off the fear that whispers in my mind. Because I already told you, fear still whispers in my mind. But I don't check inside closets and under the bed before going to sleep the way I did as a young wife. I don't neurotically check on the whereabouts of my kids, because I don't feel the need to always prepare for the worst. Instead, I actually anticipate God taking care of us.

God's got it. And he's going to prompt and alert me to action if he needs to. That's actually something my sister-in-law, Lynn, taught me. Instead of fretting about what could happen, pray for wisdom about what to do if something does happen. Good stuff. Because as you well know, bad stuff still happens all the time. God didn't promise bad stuff wouldn't happen, so he's not breaking a promise. But imagining all the bad stuff that could happen is a trap that leaves you in a wretched state of mind. Body in bed with the Enemy.

The miracle for me is, I no longer live in an anxiety-driven state of mind. No what-ifs interrupting my sleep. God can heal a mind, even one deeply infected with fear. God can untangle the worst mess and repair the way you think. Even if you've been fearing for decades.

Sometimes we, as fear-ers, need to let the truth and presence of God reboot our minds. Or maybe restore the original settings. As hard as it might be to believe, we are created *not* to fear. But we only know that kind of courage when we lean into God as our husband.

"For your Creator will be your husband; the LORD of Heaven's Armies is his name! He is your Redeemer, the Holy One of Israel, the God of all the earth."[7]

5

Close to the Cradle

After Will finished his master's degree from seminary, we gladly settled back in Austin. No more driving four hundred miles weekly, no more dual apartments. We were ready to set up house in one place with one space. Our very first home had a tiny front porch with a wooden rail covered in honeysuckle. The house sat right in the middle of a wide-angled lot with gorgeous limestone hardscape. The former owners had spent a bunch of money on that hardscape—something Will and I knew we couldn't otherwise afford on his pastor salary. But they must have run out of money after that, because they skimped on landscape. The only real highlights were a winding trail of monkey grass and a single ash tree. The lonely little tree was the main feature.

Ash trees are deciduous. They have tiny helicopter-like seeds and rounded leaves with a small, distinct point at the end. The ash tree was the only tree in our front yard. We were proud of it. Grateful for it.

Have you ever read *The Prayer Tree* by Michael Leunig? In it he writes:

The tree sends it roots beneath the surface, seeking
nourishment in the dark soil: the rich "broken down"
matter of life. As they reach down and search, the roots
hold the tree firmly to the earth.

Thus held and nourished, the tree grows upwards
into the light, drinking the sun and air and expressing
its truth: its branches and foliage, its flowers and fruit.[1]

Beautiful, isn't it? But Leunig was not writing about our ash tree. It wasn't exactly "drinking the sun and air and expressing its truth."

In the first year at our new home, the ash tree fell over during a regular-sized Texas thunderstorm. It crashed down on our knockout hardscape, leaving us with a big, broken mess of concrete. And a treeless yard. Our best guess is the ash had a weak root structure.

At twenty-three years old I had a lot in common with the ash tree. I avoided the dark, rich, broken-down matter of life. I wasn't drawing life by truly, deeply trusting God.

I didn't remember until Will reminded me years later, but during our early years of dating and marriage, I never talked about what I'd seen in junior high. I didn't talk about the fears in my head or the reasons I felt I couldn't stay home alone or that I had regular panic episodes. I literally never talked about it. As if it never happened. As if not talking about it made it disappear.

Sometimes we do that, you know? We push painful things away, never talking about them in the hope they will lose their hold on us.

My friend Heather told me she never thought much about how, when her mom and dad argued and her mom stormed out of the house, she'd worried her mom would never come home. She never told anyone she feared her mom might take her own life. She didn't discuss the confusing feelings with her dad. She didn't ask why he remained emotionless and unmoved by his wife's peculiar behavior. Instead, at only ten years old, Heather took responsibility for her three younger siblings when her mother fled, never telling anyone about her darkness until one day on the way home from a writers retreat, I inadvertently asked where her fears originated.

I guess Heather thought like I did as a young woman and

felt she didn't need to access the broken-down parts of life. I mean, who does? Who enjoys looking back at the painful pieces of the past? Who wants to look back at neglect, abuse, or violence? Who wants to dwell on past disappointments, broken relationships, or unnecessary heartbreak? Why not push forward, pray, and do the best you can? Shake it off and march onward, soldier.

I know I thought it wasn't necessary to seek a God-sourced nourishment in my history. While I prayed furiously for protection, I never prayed for wholeness. Honestly, I didn't think anything was missing in me. I thought something was missing in God—his will and resolve to keep me safe.

At twenty-three I was tentative and unsure if God was out there for me. Or for my newborn baby.

STRONGHOLDS

To say I had a stronghold of fear is an understatement. To say I was oblivious to my stronghold of fear is an enormous understatement.

I was the pregnant woman who read *What to Expect When You're Expecting*, and I followed every guideline religiously. And then I even topped their suggestions. I stopped highlighting my hair because I was scared the bleach would leach through my scalp and harm my unborn baby. I didn't eat any deli meat or pepperoni on my pizza because of the sodium nitrates. No store-bought mashed potatoes, for heaven's sake—the sulfites! I did not drink one drop of caffeine. Nope. When during my first trimester I started lightly spotting, I went nearly immobile.

I was a freak because it was all up to me. If I wanted this baby to have a fighting chance, I had to follow all the rules.

When my son, Will III, was born, my pediatrician told me the baby shouldn't be in any public place until he was at least six weeks old and had his first round of shots. No grocery store shopping, no church attendance, no running those little life-giving mommy moments at Target. He told me that if at any time our newborn developed a fever, he would take him to the children's hospital and give him a spinal tap to make sure he didn't have meningitis. He *told* me that. The doctor terrified me. So I followed all his rules. And I obeyed fear.

When my husband's college friends came to town to see the baby, I knew there was no way they could be around baby Will. It was December, the dead of winter, and they were likely carrying all kinds of flu viruses and random bacteria I hadn't even researched yet. So I let them "see" the baby through our back patio window. I am not joking. Instead of allowing them inside the house to see Will III, I had them stand on the back patio and look at him through the window. Brilliant, yes?

Before I became pregnant, I was just protecting myself. But

now that my baby was in my world, I felt completely responsible for protecting him. I willingly sacrificed anything and everything to make sure nothing bad happened to him. I didn't care what anyone thought. I wanted to be a good mom. Even if it meant bowing down to fear to get there.

Do you feel the same way about your kids? That it's your job, your responsibility, even your calling to watch over and protect and manage their world? I totally get it.

The problem with fear is, it seems a small thing to obey its voice. A small thing to allow yourself to fold your behavior around the whisper. But then fear sweeps in widespread, and suddenly you're really sick. Even obeying one tiny whisper is dangerous. It's like the little tiny tick bite that gives you Lyme disease. Widespread drama all over your body.

Thank Jesus, as Brennan Manning says, "He loves you just as you are, not as you should be."[2] God loved me. Yes. Even when I was sick and didn't know it.

SAFE NOT SICK

Deeper and deeper I dug into the dry well of fear to find the control I was seeking. Instead of leaving grocery bags at the front door while checking the closets, as I did in the early days of our marriage, I now had a child. *What to do? How can I manage both of us?* I'd make a plan.

On the days Will III and I were out running errands, if I felt the fear rising about the possibility of someone inside the house when we got home, I'd pull into my empty garage, turn off the car, and wait for the garage door to close. Then I would crack the windows and lock my baby in the car so I could check inside. Yes, lock my baby in the car—the way you secure expensive jewelry in a safe-deposit box at the bank. *Oh my.* Then with lightning speed I would literally run through the house, checking all four closets and under the bed in our little home. Then I would race back to Will III and rescue him.

Don't you see? I was his savior. Without my elaborate safety plans, something might happen to him. I couldn't handle that thought. I would do anything to protect him.

Everything was completely dependent on me. Sure, I'd shoot up prayers asking God for help. But my history told me my "safe" and God's "safe" were two different things. The racing around checking closets was about covering all my bases in case God's safe didn't cut it.

Your turn now. How do you cover the bases when God's not enough? When it's just too great a sacrifice to see if God will come through for you? How do you play the savior for the people you love? Does it in any way top my crazy? Oh, friend, I really understand. I do. It's exhausting, isn't it? Because we were never meant to be the savior of our little worlds. Never meant to carry the fears of "what-if" and "just in case."

God loves you as you are. Right here, right now. It doesn't matter how deep you are in that dry well. He's reaching in to pull you out. He's standing strong and ready to be the Savior for you and all the people you love. If God can heal me, God can heal you. Believe me.

Because Jesus is all about healing.

There is this story of Jesus and a sick man. Jesus meets the man at a pool where a bunch of sick people hang out waiting for an angelic visit and instantaneous healing. The man is a paralytic, so he is completely immobile. All he can do is lie there. Waiting. Hoping someone will help him into the healing waters. But the others are more concerned with themselves. He's feeling left behind. Forgotten. Despondent.

Jesus sees him and asks, "Do you want to get well?"

In response the guy says some stuff about his sad story, about how he can't get into the water. Jesus listens and responds, "Get up! Pick up your mat and walk."

Then the sick man picks up his mat and walks. Picks up his mat and walks! The man was cured.[3] How about that? Simple. Miraculous. Jesus.

In reading the story I see the big difference between the man and me: even though I was sick, I didn't think I was sick. I thought I was safe.

If Jesus had asked me, "Do you want to be made well?" I would have told him I wasn't sick. But I probably would have asked Jesus to make the world a safer place. I would have asked him to make all the bad people behave. I would have asked him to make sure no babies ever got fevers or meningitis. And I might have asked if he could check in all my closets, thank you very much.

In essence, I would have asked Jesus to take away the need for the broken-down matter of life. I would have asked Jesus to take away all the pain—before the pain even showed up.

I had no idea of the connection between the roots reaching into the dark and the branches reaching up to the light. No idea of the relationship between joy and despair.

Leunig summed it up for me:

Nature requires that we form a relationship between our joy and our despair, that they not remain divided or hidden from one another. For these are the feelings that must cross-pollinate and inform each other in order that the soul be enlivened and strong.[4]

I had no desire for my soul to be enlivened if it meant surrendering control or facing the darkness of my past. I certainly wasn't going to make the introduction. There would be no "Broken, messed-up Susie, meet Jesus, your Healer." If there was to be a bold place for painful feelings, it was going to be God's job. Not mine.

A Lifetime of Saturdays

If we follow the Easter story the way the church celebrates it, Jesus was tortured and hanged on a cross on Friday. His Friday was the worst kind of pain and suffering. He lay dead on Saturday. His Saturday was tomb-guarded silence. Then on Sunday . . .

Glory. Resurrection. Redemption for all of us. Jesus rose from the dead.

God is in the business of Sundays, making things come full circle in the most redemptive, beautiful way. He can do that for you too. But I think in the three-part process of Friday, Saturday, and Sunday, we often get stuck because of fear. Because fear wants to trap us in Saturday. Stick with me . . .

I think of bad things that happened in my life as Fridays. I would list these as some of my Fridays:

- witnessing the murder in the eighth grade
- watching my friend's mom getting choked by her drunken boyfriend
- hearing the story of my best friend's sister getting raped, knifed, and left for dead
- walking through a super tumultuous and sad twelve-month season in my marriage

- watching a years-long ministry friendship suffer and die
- being in a head-on car collision with a two-ton work van
- surviving eighteen months of silence from God, my dark night of the soul
- developing RSD (chronic pain disorder) following surgery after a horseback-riding incident

My Fridays are the things that bring agonizing, ongoing pain—whether physical, emotional, or spiritual. Fridays are the situations you just survive. You get through. And when they're finally over, you face Saturday.

Saturday is the "What the holy heck just happened?" kind of feeling. Equal parts grief and astonishment while trying to pick up the pieces. You may ask Saturday why, but she never answers your questions. Saturday will not return your calls or leave a trail of crumbs. Saturday makes you feel uncomfortable and spiritually awkward. Saturday just doesn't settle well into a soul.

When we are forced into communion with Saturday, we wallow in reasoning, blame, control, despondency, or denial. Saturday is not a place of wellness.

Saturday was my checking the closets because I was afraid. Saturday was feeling like I needed to be the savior of my little world. Saturday was Heather feeling responsible for her siblings because her mother was gone and her dad was present but absent. Heather and I needed healing to get to Sunday. To a life of freedom and resurrection, of redemption and childlike faith. Our souls so desperate for Sunday, and we didn't even know it. Fear locked us up in Saturday.

We can get stuck in the quiet destitution of Saturday. Sometimes for years. I was stuck for more than a decade—past the pain of bad things but not yet living in the joy of Sunday. I just wasn't ready to trust God again. I couldn't make myself pick up my mat and walk like the paralytic, because I really didn't think I was sick.

But like the paralytic, I needed to get up and walk. I needed to put one foot in front of the other, over and over, by truly trusting God again.

Is there a chance my story makes sense to you in some way? Are you choosing to be "safe and sick" instead of choosing to walk in wellness? Do you think there is even the smallest possibility you need to trust God again? Then, friend, take my hand and let's go. Let's get up and walk.

CAIRNS

Here's something I learned hiking the Rockies with my husband: hiking doesn't happen in a straight line. You don't hike straight uphill. You hike in a gently curving line, back and forth, winding up the mountain to the summit. The path looks like a much longer way to get to the top than taking it as a straight shot. Back and forth. Back and forth. Will we ever get to the top?

Maybe you're feeling that way about your life. Tired of the back-and-forth lessons in trusting God again. Tired of dealing with your painful past and worrying about your unknown future. Altogether exhausted by the mental gymnastics of following God with the voice of fear whispering in your ear. I mean, wouldn't it be great if God could just snap his fingers and heal us instantaneously? Yeah, it really would be. God *could* just snap his fingers and heal us instantaneously, but he rarely does. Instead, there is this long journey to wellness. But I think there's a reason for that: God wants intimacy with us.

I even wonder if his desire for our wholeness is all about intimacy with him. Because how can we really love him with a divided heart? Fear, with all the weirdness it brings, shoves its selfish way between God and you—and God and me. Jesus wants the closeness back. The way it was before fear showed up and shoved his ugly face into the relationship.

Now, here's something else I learned hiking with my husband: when the trail is obscure, look for cairns. Cairns are markers. Small piles of stones. When people are hiking and the path is ambiguous for whatever reason, they take small rocks off the ground and make a little mound to show you which way to go. The cairns point you to the summit trail. Isn't that the nicest thing? Hikers who came before want to help hikers coming behind. So they leave these small stone monuments to mark the way to the top.

My friend, healing from all the Fridays in life doesn't happen in a straight line. There will be lots of turns and twists along the way. I wish we could just bulldoze to the top together and sing lots of victory songs, but the truth is, it's a long, hard haul. Your feet will ache; your heart will beat faster. Hiking in the cool, thin air in the mountains will make you feel as though you're going to faint. But we'll stop together, face our downhill history, and catch our breath in amazement because we'll see we've come such a long way. We'll sip water, and when we're able to feel as if things have stopped spinning, we'll look for those markers left behind. Those little piles of cairns from other climbers in search of Sundays.

Then we will turn our eyes upward and make our tired feet move slowly up the mountain. One tiny step after another. Because we desire God—and we want the intimacy wholeness brings.

When we get to the next pile of rocks marking the way, we'll kindly pick up a small, smooth stone and place it on the pile. Grateful for those who have gone before us, praying for those who come after us. Small stones of encouragement to mark the trail.

But let's agree together that what we won't do is sit down on the path and get stuck in a decade of Saturdays. While finding healing and wholeness from all kinds of bad things is difficult, we won't camp out on the trail. We'll keep at it, by his grace, uphill all the way.

6

Flat on the Floor

I magine having a colicky newborn like my Emily, an active three-year-old like Will III, and an unsettled husband without a job. That was our situation when we moved back to Fort Worth, Texas, in 1990. Yes, back and forth from Austin to Fort Worth. We were stressed and overwhelmed. It was an absolute act of faith to move once again. Will resigned from our first-ever pastorate in Austin, our hometown, the city we both loved and the city where both our families lived. Will felt determined to complete a doctorate, and we both knew he needed to be closer to the seminary. So we agreed it was the right decision to leave our security nest known as Austin and move to Fort Worth with our two very young children.

When Will finally landed a job selling suits at Dillards, we felt relieved for the income but wondered if we'd missed hearing from God. Was this really his plan for our lives? I was sad about moving away from my family. And I didn't get how Will's selling suits represented a part of God's plan. But I followed. And then, because God seems to like last-minute things with me, we got a call to interview with the sweetest church in all of Fort Worth—Springdale Baptist Church. After a series of meetings, they offered Will the job as their pastor.

Still, our move from Austin to Fort Worth was bittersweet. I missed having my mom close to help with the babies, and I missed hanging out with my sister and her kids. The only connection and comfort for me in this new city was that I found out a dear friend from my junior high days in Austin—Cheryle— was living in Fort Worth. Yes, Cheryle, the girl who was in the classroom with me in May 1978. Now isn't that interesting? Although we hadn't connected in years, I contacted her before we moved and told her we were coming to Fort Worth, and she jumped into action. At the time we were planning our move, I was well into the last trimester of my pregnancy with Emily. So it was Cheryle who helped Will pick out a place for us to live. She found us a cute rental house just a few streets over from her own house and right next door to a park. Just perfect.

The house on Thomas Place was adorable. Three small bedrooms, one and a half baths, and a nice size kitchen/

laundry-room combo. Built in the thirties, the house still had the original hardwood floors, which were gorgeous. In the living room there stood three large floor-to-ceiling windows. Light streamed into the house all day long. But the real selling point for us was the huge backyard with a sandbox and a covered porch. Directly in the center of the yard grew a big tree we named "the butterfly tree" because throughout the year the trunk of the tree would be inexplicably covered with butterflies. This completely delighted my son.

To look out the back window at any time during the day and see butterflies, all light and fluttery, landing on the trunk of the tree was like a tiny miracle. The butterflies were attracted to an old scar on the tree. From inside the tree sticky sap oozed out the scar onto the tree's big trunk, revealing a wound that never healed.

That tree was just like me.

Oh yes, that was so me at that time in Fort Worth. An open, bleeding, gaping emotional wound. Sticky sap oozing all over the place. But in the middle of this scene, God was there, sending little love notes like butterflies, fluttering down all over my life. Gently. Gracing me.

I cry now as I think about it, big tears rolling down my cheeks, splashing on my laptop. How I didn't recognize it at the time as one more love note from God. For the excruciatingly beautiful way God loved me in my past even when I didn't see it. For the way he loves me right now as I sit here recalling this memory. He loves me in the future, scattering notes ahead on the path I've yet to see.

God loves me.

And, dear friend, God loves you.

Past. Present. Future. He loves us through it all.

He loved me all the way to Fort Worth back in 1990 so I could get well. See, I didn't know I was sick until I came to Fort Worth. I didn't even know I was sick when a friend invited me to a Bible study that very next year.

We were all young twenty-somethings, going to a Bible study hosted at the home of a seminary professor's wife. Jane was so warm and welcoming. I don't remember all she said, but I do remember her kindness and sincerity.

We were studying a book by Kay Arthur called *Lord, Heal My Hurts.* I still have that book, and right there on page thirty-three, in my own handwriting, is one little sentence:

God, if there is anything in me that needs healing, please heal me.

That, my friend, is a dangerous prayer. Do not pray that for your life if you want to keep hiding under the counter. No, do not pray that for your life if fear is your best friend and you keep anxiety close like a sister. If worry is the lens through which you experience life and you like it that way, don't ask God to heal you. Or if you're a private, introverted person and you have no intention of writing a book one day telling everyone how you used to be an anxious freak of a mother, exposing all your weirdness to the world in hopes that one other frightened fear-er might come along . . . well, don't pray the dangerous prayer. Because God takes those kinds of prayers very seriously.

God was always in process with me. I can look back over my life and see his constant company. But I believe he was waiting for me to ask him to heal me. And, oh my gracious, the floodgates burst upon the invitation. And it all started because of Jane—her availability to me as a young mother and wife, her time, her open home.

I didn't even finish the Bible study. I dropped out because it was at night, and I didn't want to be away from my family. I didn't even finish reading the book.

But God doesn't need a Bible study to heal you. He doesn't need you to finish reading this book or any other book. God, gentleman that he is, is just waiting for you to ask so he can burst in and hug you home.

YET HE IS HOLY

After I prayed that prayer, what I had braced against for decades finally happened. I began to unravel.

It started with the dangerous prayer—just a sliver of courage in trusting God again, in the thought that perhaps God knew me better than I did. And then there were conversations with Cheryle. Long mornings while we watched our boys play together at the neighborhood park and we shared a bench, both of us balancing a baby girl on our knees.

We started talking about the things that had happened in eighth grade. We talked about Mr. Grayson and the long-lasting, positive impact he'd had on our lives. We talked about John, wondering where he was and what he was doing with his life. We talked about what happened right before the murder and immediately after. And then we talked about the ways it changed us. How we lost the innocence of our childhood and our belief that the world is a safe place. How we loved God but often distrusted his plans for our lives.

Finding Cheryle again was nothing short of a miracle for me. While I longed for separation from the trauma and had distanced myself from the stigma of being a victim, I needed the companionship of understanding. A deep knowing without words. Someone who totally understood my pain and suffering and could help me sort out all the things I kept tucked inside.

Then one hot day in July there was an unusual occurrence: I managed to get both kids down for a nap at the same time. I grabbed a book and turned on some soothing, quiet music. I lay down on the floor, pillow under my head and book in hand, the afternoon sunlight streaming in through the living room windows. The patterns of the dappled light caught my attention.

Without warning, tears started streaming down my face. It was so beautiful. I took a big breath, as if I were about to go underwater. And then it happened—full-out, unexpected posttraumatic stress disorder. As I lay there, the images of the murder repeated endlessly, like a movie stuck in the most horrid replay, prying open the eyes of my soul. A boy. A gun. My teacher lying awkwardly crumpled on the floor, blood gushing out his ear.

I could hear the noise all over again. The murmuring. The gunshot. The screams. The chairs scraping on the floor. More screaming.

I could smell everything. Gunpowder. Pencils. Chalk dust. The perfume I sprayed on my T-shirt that day.

In that moment I was lost. Lost to my sense of reality. Lost to my husband and my children. Wandering in a grief so deep I thought I would never return.

I wanted to pick myself up off the floor and find home. Return to laundry, dishes, checking on my children—anything in my real life. Instead, I was transported against my will to my past. Images flashing, relentless sorrow, and a complete inability to do anything but lie on the floor and fall apart.

I thought I was going crazy.

It was a blur.

But I then heard a song, Mozart's Piano Concerto in A Major, K. 488: Adagio.

Swelling in the background, the melody was bittersweet. A lone piano, notes slow and quiet, and then strings tenderly entering, like a movie score accompanying the pictures in my head. There were more tears. I was completely caught up in the song, and then I heard a whisper. A God-reminder from my husband's sermon earlier in the week. And there were only four words:

Yet you are holy.

God . . . holy. In this confusion? Holy in these memories?

Right there on the floor, God met me and started the healing process I didn't know I needed.

The four words David spoke. Four words to catch me, comfort me. The four words God used to slowly turn me around.

Yet you are holy.

A slow revolution. The most desperate and profound soul spin.

I cried, hitting the floor with my fists over and over again, racing to escape the pain. But God suspended me through music until my mind could accept the truth.

I understood, as if for the first time, the realities in my situation were no different from those in the lives of David and Jesus. In pain they struggled with trust. They felt abandoned. David cried:

My God, my God! Why have you forsaken me?

Why do you remain so distant?

Why do you ignore my cries for help?
Every day I call to you, my God, but you do
not answer.
Every night you hear my voice, but I find
no relief.

Yet you are holy.
The praises of Israel surround your throne.[1]

In their grief there was a raw honesty I recognized, and yet they concluded the complaint with acceptance. In four little words:

Yet you are holy.

I hit replay on the song over and over again. Crying, listening, desperate to know what I needed to do with the contrast of the mental images and the Truth rising inside me.

Then finally I understood. I was to follow the example: move from grief to praise.

I had my fill of self-imposed suffering. More than a decade spent looking for closure through control. And now God was asking me to give it up. To accept the truth: No matter how things look, *God is holy*. No matter how I feel, *God is holy*. No matter how broken a woman I've become, *God is holy*.

And so with Mozart dramatically echoing across the room, I raised my voice above my tears and confessed over and over:

Yet you are holy. Yet you are holy. Yet you are holy.

God swept into the room, inhabiting my praise. A presence of comfort. Release.

And because God is also my husband—fiercely protective and unconditionally loving—he stepped in to break off my full-blown affair with anxiety. My mind was emptied of images.

The fear strapped tightly across my mind was ripped to pieces.

I lay there physically spent. I had been running in worrisome circles for years. But for the first time, joy—fragile, God-gifted joy—found a space in my now-still soul.

It was the song. It was the whisper. It was the Word.

God speaks.

The images stopped. No more of the horror roll. I was enormously relieved, but I kept crying. I realized for the first time I was the holdout. Not God. All those years listening to fear, trying to run my own life, had left me here—empty, weak, and frightened of my own faithless heart. Would I surrender my addiction of fear? Could I live without worrying? Would I lean into God as my husband, or would I try again to stand alone?

I felt more fragile than ever.

Unsure whether I could actually trust myself to trust God, I felt spiritually frail even in the face of this obvious God-visit. Could I step out of who I was and into who I needed to be?

Could I live my life with my face up, hands outstretched to a God who is loving but mysterious? A Father who is holy and perfect but allows his children to live in an unsafe world?

Could I actually live unafraid?

ARE YOU LISTENING?

It's scary, isn't it? The idea of living unafraid in an unsafe world. I really wish God didn't expect that kind of trust from us. But he does. He asks us to trust him completely every single day in every single way. And sometimes that just feels like too much.

Sure, when everything is going according to our plans, it's easy. Trusting God is actually fun. It's a "Thank you, God, for making my life so beautiful." But when you're single and waiting for a husband, afraid you'll be alone all your life, it's not so nice. Or when you're unemployed and can't provide for your family because you're waiting for a job, it's not so fun to trust God. When you're cuddling the baby you prayed for, trust is a marvel. But when you're dealing with the heartbreak of years of infertility and you're visiting a friend cuddling her new baby, trusting God hurts. Deeply.

It is a challenge to trust God, to live unafraid in the face of trials and trouble and heartache. No doubt God knew we would struggle with this since he talks about it cover to cover in his Word. So my struggle—and maybe yours too—is how to simply trust God when I feel afraid. How to release the stronghold of fear, the addiction to anxiety. How to get that kind of childlike trust.

It's a really big question with answers splintering out in a million different directions. But I do know this: there's no room for childlike trust if you don't think trust is necessary. There's no reason to lean into God if you're leaning into yourself, as I did for more than a decade.

As a young child, when I got bored in church, one of the things I'd do to distract myself was find the middle page in the *Baptist Hymnal*. I'd hold the hymnal in my lap and start at both ends, moving page by page to find the song in the center. One of the things my pastor, Dr. Smith, used to do to capture the attention of kids like me was to stop the sermon, right in the middle, and ask, "Are you listening? Are you listening to me?"

Without fail, every time I heard his booming voice asking, "Are you listening? Are you listening to me?" I'd stop what I was doing and listen to Dr. Smith.

I think there are times in life God does the same thing. Times when he stops everything we are doing to make sure we are listening. Certainly he was stopping everything for me, asking me to listen in the middle of my "Yet you are holy" moment.

And, gracious, let me reemphasize, as hard as it was—God

was so kind and good to me. By allowing me to revisit those images, God was doctoring my soul. Reviving my spirit. Though that moment came crashing in loud and unexpectedly, it was necessary for my healing.

In the book of Acts, Paul definitely had an "Are you listening?" moment with God. It was obtrusive. It was loud. It was so dramatic, in fact, that Paul didn't eat or drink anything for three days afterward. During that time Paul was blind.[2] He couldn't see a thing while Jesus was "giving him by his Spirit a full view of himself."[3]

I guess the similarity here between Paul and me is that we had no idea who we really were and what was driving us on the inside. No awareness of our spiritual condition before a holy God.

While these moments, these avenues of communication, aren't usually what we're looking for—because they're often painful—they're essential so we can see ourselves as we really are. Who knows how long I would have continued to think I was safe, not sick, if God hadn't allowed my PTSD to fall full force on my life and crush me into dependence on him? Who knows how long I would have held tightly to fear as my savior? But God—in his love and tender mercy—allowed the hurt to bring healing. He lifted his hand, letting the memories flood out so I could see where I needed to be to get well and find peace in Jesus.

There is no peace outside of Jesus. No rest for those weary souls running from pain if not in God.

Is there a chance you are tired of running, ready for rest in God? Well, you're in good company, friend. There are lots of fellow strugglers—fear-ers ready to give God a second chance with their lives, working out the reality that God is completely trustworthy even though he left us in an unsafe world.

If we could only talk about it honestly.

7

Crying Out Loud

A small grove of aspen trees sits clustered next to our family cabin in Estes Park, Colorado. My father-in-law—we call him G-dad—protects the grove. He waters it. He fenced in the small colony with green netting to keep the elk from stripping the tender bark. My favorite time to see the aspen grove is in autumn, when the leaves flutter like golden butterflies against the cool, blue sky.

The thing I didn't know about aspen until G-dad told me is that a single seed actually produces a whole colony of trees. That's why you never see a solitary aspen tree. No lone-ranger aspen on the side of a mountain. Instead, there are always large groups of the trees. You'll even see acres of aspen winding their way up the mountains. It's one enormous root system that connects them so tightly. A grove of aspen can survive all kinds of trauma, even forest fires, because of the unique root structure. The strength of the aspen is the tree's community.

The strength of my life during my posttraumatic stress was my community, a small group of moms meeting in a family room. We were neighbors and friends, clustered together, connected by our love of God. Women I knew only because my friend Cheryle was nice enough to bring me along. These women who were her friends became my friends. They helped me see God's truth and comfort in my little life there on Thomas Place.

It wasn't anything specific they said to help me. No big Bible promises. No preachy-teachy reasons why I was falling apart. They offered unconditional acceptance in a time and place that was utter chaos for me—a spiritual and emotional grief so deep I was unable to wade out without their help.

I remember the day I decided to tell my small group what I was going through. I had talked it all out with Cheryle, and she encouraged me to open up to the group. I came in, sat down, and we got started. I listened to my new friends talking about their stuff. One woman talked about her concerns for her marriage. One talked again about her panic attacks when driving and how she couldn't go over bridges. She didn't know why. The doctor's wife felt she couldn't manage the kids and the schedule and the loneliness. Here were these women pouring out their hearts to each other.

In our past meetings I'd say something I thought was helpful. I'd try to encourage. But in this meeting I just sat there trying to hold it all in, wondering if I was going to burst, waiting my turn. And it happened. I exploded with all kinds of information about myself they'd never heard. I told them about the murder Cheryle and I had witnessed and about my posttraumatic stress attack—how I lay on the floor, completely out of control. I cried, telling them about how my brain felt like a shattered window and how I worried I'd never be able to gather all the pieces and put it back together again. I just cried and cried.

And they sat there quietly listening. I was no Susie Sunshine. I wasn't the person I usually was in small group. I was messy. Unsure. Uncomposed. Wrecked. I couldn't catch my breath when I tried to talk through the tears. I couldn't make sense of what I was trying to tell them. My mind was still recalling the memories, and I couldn't think clearly. I was muddled. Distracted. I was doing laundry, planning meals, and taking care of my children—but just barely. I told them everything that had happened the week before when I was on the floor crying.

And they listened. Quietly. Carefully. Then they did something beautiful. They didn't judge or preach or try to tell me everything was going to be okay. They just let me be. All broken in that place. Then they prayed for me. And they held me.

Community.

When You Stop Running

Something happens when we are willing to be real with other people about our lives, when we are open to acknowledging our stories. We receive comfort. We grow courage. We are the Church.

For a very long time I ran from the all the scary things that had happened to me. Too afraid to look back and honestly accept the pain. Too hyped up on fear to know the truth of how my story impacted where I was in life. It was just too big and too hard. Until the day I could no longer keep it all packed inside of me.

The day I hit the floor, with Mozart filling the room, was the day God called me out of my affair with fear. It was both painful and beautiful. I felt horrified and relieved that the secret was out. The first person to know about this was my husband. I called him to come home during my first PTSD episode. I told him that I thought I was breaking apart and that I couldn't handle the kids. Will rushed home to find me crying on the floor.

For better or for worse.

I lay there spent, saying, "I don't know what's happening to me. I can't control my mind. I'm broken." More sobbing.

Then Will, ever the man, said, "We'll get through this."

Later that night when we were in bed, my head aching as if it were in a vice, I complained to Will, "How come nothing bad ever happened to you?" And then Will proceeded to tell me some things that had happened to him. Things we'd never talked about, like how he drank a fifth of whiskey at thirteen years old—alone—and then threw up over the balcony outside his window and passed out. When I asked why in the world he was drinking a fifth of whiskey, alone, at thirteen, more of his life spilled out. Things I never knew.

How were we married for seven years and never before got to the place we could talk about all the dark stuff? I think it's because we didn't want to. At some point we both believed the lie that if you don't talk about it, it really doesn't have a hold on you. If you don't revisit the sad, weird, confusing stuff in your life, you're over it.

Okay. So I'm going to ask the question you probably don't want to hear: Is there sad, weird, confusing stuff in your life that you've never talked about? Things that just might be impacting where you are in life, how you think and act? Are there behaviors controlling you that you don't really understand but which might be linked to an event or series of events in your past? Does it make you feel gross just thinking about it? Like you want to snap the top down before something creeps out and slimes your present reality? Does it make you want to slam down this book?

I know. I really do, because I lived like that for so long. Running from my past. Afraid if I stopped running long enough to look back and assess, I'd get completely run over and never recover.

Brené Brown[1] said, "Owning our story can be hard but not nearly as difficult as spending our lives running from it. Embracing our vulnerabilities is risky but not nearly as dangerous as giving up on love and belonging and joy—the experiences that make us the most vulnerable. Only when we are brave enough to explore the darkness will we discover the infinite power of our light."[2]

The night Will and I began talking about all the things in our lives that were dark and hurtful was a turning point in our marriage. If I hadn't fallen apart, I wouldn't have been healed from the hurtful things in my life—and neither would've Will.

I'm grateful Will allowed me to be vulnerable, to completely fall apart and let God put me back together. And so did the moms' small group. I had people in my life who gave me the love and space to own my narrative, even though I felt it was overwhelming and ugly. When I was open with them about the true things happening in my life—open about the darkness—I was comforted. Because I allowed myself to mourn.

MOURNING

Mourning is expressing grief out loud. Jesus did that. He modeled it for us.

When the stress and all the affective pain of knowing he was going to die was sitting on Jesus, he didn't escape it. Instead, he gathered three friends, went to the Garden of Gethsemane, and faced the inevitable.

> Then Jesus came with them to a place called Gethsemane, and said to His disciples, "Sit here while I go over there and pray." And He took with Him Peter and the two sons of Zebedee, and began to be grieved and distressed. Then He said to them, "My soul is deeply grieved, to the point of death; remain here and keep watch with Me."
>
> And He went a little beyond them, and fell on His face and prayed, saying, "My Father, if it is possible, let this cup pass from Me; yet not as I will, but as You will." And He came to the disciples and found them sleeping, and said to Peter, "So, you men could not keep watch with Me for one hour?"[3]

Jesus moved toward his crucifixion and death—and he moved toward it with his friends. The Bible says he set his face resolutely toward Jerusalem.[4] Purposefully toward pain and suffering. Completely open to his unfolding narrative. With "boldness, courage, constancy and firmness of mind."[5]

If I were Jesus, I probably would have canceled my small group that week. I wouldn't have wanted to have dinner with the disciples. Especially Judas. And I certainly wouldn't have wanted to take three of my closest friends to the Garden of Gethsemane only to have them fall asleep on me.

Jesus mourned in the garden. Sadly, he mourned alone. But I guess the whole point of this is that Jesus sought community. And he wanted it, knowing he would be completely real in his narrative, entirely open to mourning with his people. Even if his people let him down.

While I thought I was a very open kind of person at twenty-eight, mourning was new to me. Mourning is so super vulnerable that it's embarrassing. And messy. Not something for those of us who care about image management. Mourning is not something you're likely to schedule into your day, but when mourning knocks, if you want to be healthy, it would be wise to open the door.

In that small group I cried over losing a big chunk of my childhood to the murder. I cried over its impact on my life as a young wife. I mourned the fact that the whole situation had made me a freakish, fearing mother.

For me, mourning with those women was about pulling

out all the deeply buried ideas I had of God and spilling them onto the coffee table, telling my friends I loved God but didn't trust him with my life—or my children's lives. It was saying out loud, "I feel our safety is all up to me. And I feel that is too big to handle. I feel as if I am breaking. Literally breaking apart."

People like me who don't mourn over bad things, sad things—whatever-life-throws-at-you things—end up anxious and depressed on the inside. To better manage those feelings, we end up creating systems apart from God. I chose hyper-control. Some people choose to forget with alcohol or food. Others pick suffering as a mode of operation—a kind of every-day helplessness. It's all the same thing, I think. Blocked-up sadness. Poverty in spirit.

I am so un-Jesus-y about pain. Are you? First off, I don't want to step into it or toward it, and, second, I'd rather not have any pain at all. That way I could just meet for happy hour with my friends and laugh about the good stuff in life. No need for gathering in small groups for the purpose of walking out the hard stuff in life.

Maybe that's where you are—avoiding the dark, painful stuff. I totally get it. It feels smart and productive to skim over all the negativity. It even seems a bit spiritual to gloss over the past, denying its reach into the future, and yet the Bible says something different.

God blesses those who are poor and realize
    their need for him,
      for the Kingdom of Heaven is theirs.
God blesses those who mourn,
    for they will be comforted.[6]

It's the poor in spirit, the mourners, who get comfort and blessing. Not the hard workers or the avoiders. That's crazy upside down to me, but it's what Jesus said. And I know he, of all people, would know the truth about that one.

COLLECTING TEARS

It takes a lot of courage to be truthful. To let people know you're a mess on the inside—and get your grief out loud. And it feels ridiculously lonely when you're in the middle of it. But, of course, you're never alone, because God promises he will never leave or forsake you.[7] Not when you feel like a mess. Not when you feel you have it all together.

God gathers our tears.[8] Collects them, counts them, bottles them up. He has unending love for us and empathy for our situation. If he wanted, he could swoop right down and hug us tight in real time and whisper that things will be all right. But instead, he chose regular ol' people to comfort us in the middle of our hard times. He picked people like you and me as dispensers of his tender mercy.

There are times we need a hug. A prayer. A listening ear. The tricky part is that it's not always easy to know when those times will come along. So God made a plan for us to gather, to not neglect meeting together.[9] That happens in church, at Sunday school, and in Bible studies, and it happens in our homes—those times when we regularly gather to strengthen the spiritual safety net we all need.

Since I'm an introvert, I have a tendency to hide out. To stay home clustered with my family. And that is all. But I learned an important lesson in my Fort Worth moms' group. Gathering with other believers is not optional for me, because I know that no matter how I'm feeling about my life, I'm always a step away from becoming a doubter and a two-timing lover with God again. Much as an alcoholic realizes her absolute addiction to alcohol, I understand this pull I have to fear. Quite simply, I'm not strong enough to stand on my own.

The Enemy knows right where to hit me, the right buttons to push. So I don't have the luxury to walk out life alone. I need people. Even though I'm an introvert. Even though my job as a writer requires lots of solitude. Even though my role as a pastor's wife sometimes makes me want to run far, far away from expectation and disappointment. I need people. And so do you, friend.

I wish we could start a little online group. A Former Fearers Anonymous sort of thing. But truly, I need people sitting in my family room. I need three or four who see me where I live, at the grocery store, in my roles as pastor's wife, mother, sister, daughter. People who really know me. People who can comfort me, hug me, pray with me, and give me a kick in the butt when I need it.

DARK NIGHT OF THE SOUL

I mentioned at the beginning that God talks to me. I know that sounds weird, but he really does talk to me in the smallest and most personal ways—and always has.

When I'm sitting in traffic feeling completely overwhelmed, and I see fuzzy cottonwood seeds floating over the hood of my car, I don't think it's random. I know that's God reminding me of the cottonwood tree he had my dad plant at Murchison Junior High. He's encouraging me, reminding me he's still in control even when I feel I'm in over my head. Deeply personal and delightfully creative. Or when, on one of my saddest days ever, yellow finches suddenly showed up on the feeders in my backyard after I'd spent three years filling Niger seed in special finch feeders and then had waited and waited for them. That was God speaking hope to me, sending a love note saying, *Hey,*

I'm still looking out for you. Beautiful things are ahead. I believe in those little yellow finch love notes.

God had always talked to me in tangible ways, until the summer of 2007, when God went quiet.

I didn't notice it at first. A couple of days went by without any notes or noise. Then suddenly I realized it had been a week. Then two. And that's when I implored God to speak. To say something. Anything. I thought maybe sin was creating the distance, so I asked for forgiveness of anything and everything I could think of . . . but still there was quiet. I kept praying. Continually. And then I started asking around. Was God going quiet on everyone? No. Apparently not.

Just me.

It was horrible—honestly one of the worst things I've been through. I was so scared. Worried God would never speak to me again. I remember driving thirty minutes to the barn to ride my horse and having to pull off the highway because I was crying so hard. Trying to get big gulps of air, my tears like an ocean, overwhelming and drowning me. The loneliness was so intense. So heavy. What did I do? Why was God silent?

I identified deeply with Job when he asked God, "Am I a burden to you?"[10] Over and over in my journal, I cried out to God, *Am I a burden to you? Am I a burden to you? Am I a burden to you? What have I done to you, O watcher of humanity?*[11]

I wept every time I met with my friends Jillynn and Erika. We had a weekly prayer group at the time just to check in and pray for each other. Every week they'd come over, and every week I'd cry. They didn't know what to say to me. They didn't have answers for why God stood so still and quiet. It was as if I were in a small, dark closet. Under the door I could see light. It was God. He stood on the other side of the door. But he would not come in. And I couldn't get out. That went on for months.

I was so sad that I was convinced I needed an anti-depressant. So I went to our counselor friend, Rick. I told him everything, and he looked up and said, "You don't need an antidepressant. You're in a dark night of the soul. All the ancients talk about it."

To be diagnosed with something was spectacular. Because then the problem could be solved, right? I read everything I could find on the dark night of the soul and felt somewhat encouraged by gaining information. We do that. We fill ourselves with information when we hurt, when we're confused, when we're afraid. As if knowing things will make things better.

Then I found Mother Teresa's journal entries in *Come Be My Light.* I got to certain portions of the book and sobbed uncontrollably.

Please pray for me, that it may please God to lift this darkness from my soul for only a few days. For sometimes the agony of desolation is so great and at the same time the longing for the Absent One so deep, that the only prayer which I can still say is—Sacred Heart of Jesus I trust in Thee—I will satiate Thy thirst for souls.[12]

I could identify with her. God went quiet on her. When I reached the end of the book, fully expecting a happy ending, it was the worst information ever. Because. God. Never. Spoke. To. Her. Again. *Ever.*

I really fell apart at our next small group meeting, completely terrified that God, as he did with Mother Teresa, would not speak to me ever again. Scared that God would never open the closet door but would only stand on the other side listening to me sob. Jillynn and Erika sat with me while I cried. The Jesus in them sitting close to me.

While I was crying out for communication, God's plan for my comfort, his very real hug, was sitting right next to me. Week after week Jillynn and Erika would show up at my house. Week after week they would sit beside me, being the Church. They never rolled their eyes or implored me to stop crying. They never were short tempered about my spiritual condition. Instead, week after week they would show up on my doorstep.

Looking back I now realize God was communicating—

through Jillynn and Erika. Yellow-finch comfort in my dark night of the soul. God spoke to me . . . through community.

It might amuse you to know God started "talking" to me again in the manner I was accustomed to about nine months later. I stopped at McDonald's to pick up a small coffee. When I went to add cream to the coffee, I thought maybe I'd take an extra packet or two home because I happen to love McDonald's creamers, and I heard God say in the nicest, most amusing way, *You don't need those extra creamers.*

Astonished at finally hearing his voice again, I laughed out loud.

TRANSITIONS

Fear is a wild weed with deep roots. I wish I could tell you that all I had to do to get well back in Fort Worth was tell my small group. To open up and expose my affair with fear to my friends. But God is jealous. He doesn't just want to cut off the top parts of the wild weed we see in our lives; he wants the deep, entangled roots out too. The places where fear runs out of control, strangling trust. While I truly felt that opening up to my small group in Fort Worth was the big finale—the end of my fear exposé— there was still more God would do to bring me to wholeness. Things I never dreamed I would have the courage to withstand.

8

A Big Misunderstanding

The upheaval of having posttraumatic stress in Fort Worth made me think back over my life a lot. Every day there'd be a new, and usually unwelcome, memory.

Some memories involved my friends. I remembered that during my freshman year in high school, my friend Laura came over when my parents weren't home. Something startled me. Scared me. Triggered a panic attack. I grabbed her arm and ran to my closet. We fell down on top of my platform shoes, pompoms, and metal hangers and sat crumpled in the dark.

"I hear something," I whispered.

She listened for a minute and then said, "I don't hear anything. I don't think there's anything to worry about."

"No, shh. Be quiet. Wait." I kept a tight grip on her arm, trying to squeeze the terror into her so she would take the fear seriously.

We waited a few more minutes. No sounds. Nothing to cause alarm.

Finally she asked, "How long do we have to stay here?"

Startled out of my panic by the clarity of her question, I pushed open the closet door.

Some memories I alone owned. During my sophomore year in high school, whenever I'd go for a run, I'd have to make a choice: downhill past the school where the murder took place or uphill past the house of the boy who murdered my teacher. My house was forever stuck in between. I usually went uphill, because it led to an easy two-mile loop. But every time I went past John's house, I wondered if he would shoot me through one of his big picture windows.

It may sound paranoid, but for me it seemed a real possibility because John never went to jail. Since he was only thirteen years old when he killed our teacher, a diagnosis of schizophrenia kept him out of a correctional facility. Good for him, not so good for me, because I had no idea where he was. Rumor had it that he made his home in Highland Park, an affluent area of Dallas, with his psychiatrist. But many times I heard he had headed back to Austin to visit his family. This scared me senseless.

When I went jogging up my street, I'd pick up the pace as

I reached his house. A large southern magnolia tree, a gift to his family from Lady Bird Johnson, sat in his front yard. John's dad worked for LBJ, and the tree came all the way from Washington, DC. It didn't matter much to me where the tree came from. As long as it blocked the view, I was grateful. Like somehow it protected me.

What a joke, thinking a magnolia tree could save me. Sure, the tree produces the most fragrant flowers ever—white showy wonders nestled in glossy green leaves—but could it act as some kind of personal bulletproof vest? A tree can't provide protection from bad things. Right?

Nothing kept me safe from the bad things. Not God, not my parents, and certainly not my neighbor's tree. At sixteen I understood that life was pretty much out of control. And there's not much else to do but protect yourself the best you're able—and keep begging God to pay attention.

PROTECTING YOURSELF

Since I felt God was a sideline observer in the bigger areas of my life, I gave John an awful lot of credit for my life history. I figured John wrecked my life at fourteen. He walked in with that rifle and blew away my childhood, my sense of safety, and my hope for a happily ever after. It was John who stood in the way of hope and a future.

I had no idea I was holding unforgiveness over John. I figured the facts were the facts, thank you very much. He walked in and wrecked a lot of people's lives that day in May 1978.

The tricky thing about unforgiveness is that it creates strongholds. Fortresses so powerful and so deceptive they seem normal. And they feel normal.

For me it was normal to consider John the problem. To have righteous indignation over the fact that he didn't get punished and was living off and on at home during high school. To wonder how in the world he ended up attending a prestigious university and then going on to get a law degree. The math didn't add up for me. And it didn't add up for other people either. Plenty of others in my life were quick to express astonishment over the situation.

Staying mad at John was a way to protect myself. And in many ways it seemed an avenue to honor my teacher's life. If I forgave John, I thought it would condone what he did to Mr. Grayson, his wife, his baby, and everyone else impacted by the madness of the situation.

But that's not really the way it works.

Unforgiveness is a hot coal in your hand. The longer you hold it, the longer it burns. You quickly go from first- to second- to third-degree burns without even realizing how the ember is eating away at the layers of your skin. And even after you drop the hot coal, your flesh still burns. It takes something radical to counteract the process.

HONEST WAGE

There is a song by Penny & Sparrow called "Honest Wage," which really bothers me. Every time I hear it, it unsettles me. Especially this lyric:

> I wish it was easier to kiss you on the mouth,
> like it is to work hard and earn an honest wage.
> But you're not always fair to me. Like I wish
>   you would be.
> He's the one who left home, I'm the one who
>   stayed.[1]

It's based on the story in the book of Luke about two brothers. Two brothers and their father. The younger brother decides to leave the family—with his inheritance. He leaves without considering his dad's feelings. He's off. Gone. No one hears from him. He breaks his dad's heart with his choices and his silence.

The other brother stays close to the father and the family. Works hard, earns an honest wage. He is steady and dependable and fulfills the role of a "good" son. He thinks he and his dad are a good team. They're on the same page.

And then it happens. The younger brother shows up broke and dirty and needy, and what does the dad do? Runs to him. Embraces him. Kisses him.

And the clincher? He throws a party for him.

How does the older brother feel? Angry. Cheated. Indignant.

The whole story is worth a read from the Word:

Then he said, "There was once a man who had two sons. The younger said to his father, 'Father, I want right now what's coming to me.'

"So the father divided the property between them. It wasn't long before the younger son packed his bags and left for a distant country. There, undisciplined and dissipated, he wasted everything he had. After he had gone through all his money, there was a bad famine all through that country and he began to hurt. He signed on with a citizen there who assigned him to his fields to slop the pigs. He was so hungry he would have eaten the corncobs in the pig slop, but no one would give him any.

"That brought him to his senses. He said, 'All those farmhands working for my father sit down to three meals a day, and here I am starving to death. I'm going back to my father. I'll say to him, Father, I've sinned against God, I've sinned before you; I don't deserve to be called your son. Take me on as a hired hand.' He got right up and went home to his father.

"When he was still a long way off, his father saw him. His heart pounding, he ran out, embraced him, and kissed him. The son started his speech: 'Father, I've sinned against God, I've sinned before you; I don't deserve to be called your son ever again.'

"But the father wasn't listening. He was calling to the servants, 'Quick. Bring a clean set of clothes and dress him. Put the family ring on his finger and sandals on his feet. Then get a grain-fed heifer and roast it. We're going to feast! We're going to have a wonderful time! My son is here—given up for dead and now alive! Given up for lost and now found!' And they began to have a wonderful time.

"All this time his older son was out in the field. When the day's work was done he came in. As he approached the house, he heard the music and dancing. Calling over one of the houseboys, he asked what was going on. He told him, 'Your brother came home. Your father has ordered a feast—barbecued beef!—because he has him home safe and sound.'

"The older brother stalked off in an angry sulk and

119

refused to join in. His father came out and tried to talk to him, but he wouldn't listen. The son said, 'Look how many years I've stayed here serving you, never giving you one moment of grief, but have you ever thrown a party for me and my friends? Then this son of yours who has thrown away your money on whores shows up and you go all out with a feast!'

"His father said, 'Son, you don't understand. You're with me all the time, and everything that is mine is yours—but this is a wonderful time, and we had to celebrate. This brother of yours was dead, and he's alive! He was lost, and he's found!' "[2]

The older brother misunderstood his father's heart. That is what made it so hard for him to see his younger brother back at home. He made assumptions that were inconsistent with who their dad was and how he felt about the younger brother. The older brother figured that after his brother grabbed the money and left the family, his dad would disown him. He thought his younger brother's whoring around would divide his father's heart. The older brother mistakenly believed there were things the younger brother could do to obliterate his father's affection.

It's exactly what I did with God.

I figured John and I were on separate teams because John did something really bad. Something unforgettable and unforgivable. I thought I was on the good team and John was on the bad team. I believed God didn't like the bad team. I thought that when God looked at John, he had his arms crossed and his brow furrowed.

I managed to get John's sin mixed up with John himself. And somehow I managed to completely forget my sin was equal to John's in God's eyes. Until one day when I was in the shower getting ready for church and a good old hymn I memorized in my childhood came racing back at me.

What can wash away my sin?
Nothing but the blood of Jesus;
What can make me whole again?
Nothing but the blood of Jesus.

Oh! precious is the flow
That makes me white as snow;
No other fount I know,
Nothing but the blood of Jesus.[3]

A shower, a song, and a Holy Spirit invasion made me understand: we were on the same team, John and I. God didn't have his arms crossed when he looked at John. He had his arms open wide. Kisses for both of us.

For God so loved the world—including John—that he

gave his Son, Jesus. The Jesus I fell in love with at twelve years old. The Jesus I couldn't shake even though I felt in many ways he stood powerless in the arena of my personal protection. That Jesus. He died. For me. And for John. Just the same.

It was then I realized I had unforgiveness toward John. I had pushed away from the family table like the older brother—standing apart from the Father because of my hurt. When I stopped pointing an angry finger at John, I could see for the first time that I had made my own choices over how I handled the tragedy. I ran from the source of healing and wholeness all on my own—from the minute John walked out of the classroom in May 1978 until some eighteen years later—a prodigal in my own right.

Tears running down my cheeks, water rushing off my back, I was freed for the first time from all the anger I held against John. Released from the bitterness I held against God for letting John do it. Choking back those words as if I heard them for the first time: *Nothing but the blood of Jesus.*

All those years hooked on anxiety never once allowed me to think about how John felt after the murder or what might have become of his mind, heart, and spirit. I never considered where he might be standing in relation to God.

The realization crushed me. I forgave John. Right there in the shower, God gave an invitation and I accepted.

AUDACIOUS FORGIVENESS

The problem with unforgiveness is that it's fear based. Holding unforgiveness is a sure sign you're afraid of getting hurt again. Maybe you can relate and you're on guard against the friend who slandered you, the boss who lied to your face, or the kid in your son's fifth grade class whose merciless teasing reduced your child to tears day after day. Or possibly it's the doctor who misdiagnosed your symptoms, creating all kinds of unnecessary and uncomfortable implications. I don't have to think these things up. They happen to you and me all the time.

The deal with holding on to unforgiveness is that it makes you defensive. You develop an excessive sensitivity to the offense. Walls up. Punchy. You're always concentrating on and sizing up the opposition to keep them from getting to you, protective of the hole they stabbed in your heart. But defensiveness is a cover for anxiety. We keep our guard up to keep something bad from happening again.

The problem is, we become protective of a weakness inside of us, making the offense disproportionate. If unforgiveness is driving a relational situation for you, count on becoming weaker, not stronger. The longer you hold on to the issue, the more likely it is to make you fragile and crumbly. Don't get me wrong. Get angry as you ought to over the injustice. Do what's necessary in the situation, and then offer forgiveness. Whether in your mind between you and God, as I did with John—or in person, face to face. The Bible says: "Be angry, and yet do not sin; do not let the sun go down on your anger, and do not give the devil an opportunity."[4]

Forgiveness obliterates a foothold for the devil.

In my situation there was only one big thing to forgive—the murder. For many other people, like my friend Brandy, forgiveness becomes an ongoing, years-long process.

Brandy and her husband really loved each other, and they had two boys. But for many years Brandy's husband kept a secret: he had cheated on her. It was a devastating blow when she found out. They went to counseling. He was remorseful and they reconciled, but he ended up cheating again, this time with a different woman. Brandy and her husband divorced.

In a situation like this, I would be crazy. Livid. I would probably hold a grudge the size of Texas . . . but I'm not Brandy.

Brandy wholeheartedly forgave her husband. Not only that, she forgave the woman who ended up becoming her husband's second wife. Brandy had compassion for the new wife, who wasn't a Christian, so she prayed for her. And eventually she shared Christ with his new young wife. When the new wife became a Christian, Brandy baptized her. And months later when the new wife started realizing the mess she'd made of herself and the family, it was Brandy who counseled her through it and urged her to stick with the marriage.

This kind of audacious, ongoing forgiveness is not easy for me. I immensely respect people like Brandy who have learned to extend forgiveness over and over again. People like Brandy remind me of King David in the Bible.

God anointed David as king when he was just a teenager. For more than a decade, he waited until the time came to step up into kingship. In the meantime the existing king, Saul, horribly mistreated him. Saul stalked, abused, and slandered David. He chased David from his homeland—the very country and people God anointed him to rule. Saul even tried to kill David.

David had a lot to be scared of for a very long time. I think fear was probably a stronghold in his life. If you look back over the Bible at the way David prayed in the psalms, you'll see it was almost always about protection. He talked a lot about fear. I imagine he dealt with panic attacks. I bet the what-ifs swarmed around him like angry bees. And yet . . .

He was brave—and he was tender, constantly positioning himself in an attitude of courage and forgiveness toward Saul. David rejected an opportunity to kill Saul, and most would have felt the action was in self-defense. But he didn't.[5] Instead, he continued to forgive Saul. This is the stuff of real heroes.

David lived a victorious kind of life despite all the bad things Saul brought into his life. Just as Brandy did with her husband.

Forgiveness makes you stronger, not weaker.

Up All Night

I don't understand the spiritual mechanics of forgiveness, but I do know the tsunami effect it had on my life. Forgiveness is a powerful thing. After forgiving John, I started seeing things differently for the first time. My PTSD eased considerably. And my thinking about God and fear began to break open.

I remember so clearly one bright afternoon a few days after the forgiveness ambush. I had just finished perusing a fabric store with my kids, trying to find something new to recover our worn sofa. I loaded both kids into the car. Will III climbed into the backseat of our suburban. Then I buckled Emily, only two at the time, in her car seat. I got into our Suburban and started driving toward home. And I had one of those crazy, almost audible spiritual messages. One of the clearest I've ever had. I heard God say, *Being afraid doesn't keep you safe. I keep you safe.*

Winding through our neighborhood on a ten-minute drive toward home thinking about what God had said, I realized I'd had a master's-level class in about two seconds. And somehow it stuck. I believed. And I decided to look to God for safety instead of following fear.

Now it doesn't mean that in two seconds all my fears were gone. Not at all. Ridiculous things still rolled around in my head, but the day I heard God I started fighting fear instead of following fear. I started standing up to fear instead of cowering. I held on to the truth: it is God who keeps me safe, not fear. That bright, sunny day I started changing my behaviors. Unlocking my mental muscle memory. Trying to pick apart the ways I thought and did life. It wasn't easy, but it was a start.

One of the first brave steps was staying in the house overnight—without Will.

Will left to attend a conference at Willow Creek Community Church near Chicago and would be gone for two nights. So it was just the kids and me at the house. My usual fear-based plan was to pack up the kids and head to Austin and stay with my folks. Or I'd call my mom or a friend to come stay with us. But this time I knew I needed to try it alone.

It wasn't pretty that first night. When both kids were tucked in safely, I pulled some blankets out and made a cozy spot on the sofa. Then I stayed up all night doing needlepoint in the family room and listening to praise music and Mozart. That might sound like a cop-out to you. But to me it was enormous. Being able to stay by myself was huge.

Sure I felt like throwing up the next day because I didn't

sleep all night, but I managed to get a nap that afternoon while the kids slept. I was doubly exhausted the next night, but I knew I needed to try it again. I fell asleep off and on all night between sewing sessions. And hey, I finished a whole Beatrix Potter needlepoint rabbit for Emily. But when the first morning light peeked through the family-room window, success smiled my way—a huge hurdle overcome. For me, it was p-r-o-d-u-c-t-i-v-e. I learned to follow God to freedom, one dark night at a time.

It starts like this for most fear-ers: one dark night at a time. Just baby steps. Small changes reflecting big courage. Creeping out from under the counter and reclaiming territory previously owned by the Enemy.

We can do this, you and I. No matter if you're locked in unforgiveness, tangling with the devil's favorite foothold, or stuck in old patterns molded in memories from years back. We offer up all our weaknesses to a big God. The One who equips us to face things we never dreamed we could.

9

Back on the Scene

Two momentous things happened in the spring of 1993. Our youngest child, Sara, came into the world bright and happy. We called her the angel baby of life. Sara completed our family of five. Ten days later another something new came into our lives. Will and I decided to leave our healing home in Fort Worth and move back to Austin to start a church. We packed up our black-and-gray Suburban and headed four hours south. Will and I were thrilled to be in our hometown again near our extended families—a little apprehensive about income and insurance but grateful. Leaving our Baptist roots, we decided to start something new all on our own. Austin Christian Fellowship was founded in the family room of our friends' home.

We prayed everything in—from a meeting place for the church to a place for our family to live. While Will was busy working to make ACF functional, I was intent on finding the perfect house for our young family. I had a list of five requirements: a one-story, three-bedroom home, located in the neighborhood I grew up in, with a flat driveway for the kids to ride their tricycles on, and a big backyard. In a matter of weeks, God miraculously said yes to the whole list.

We moved into our little dream home, an older, ranch-style brick house with a huge sycamore tree in the front yard. While the house looked neat and tidy, the big sycamore made a mess of things. The tree shed enormous leaves—ten to twelve inches in size—that littered the yard and concealed the grass underneath. Massive flakes of bark fell off the tree, leaving a pile at the base. Sycamores have big, irregular pieces of the trunk that continually fall off and leave the smooth underside of the bark exposed. The exposed portion is beautiful and smooth. A gorgeous green-gray color. If you're not familiar with sycamores, you might think this process means the tree is sick. It's not at all, though. Sycamores just let us see the growth process better because their bark isn't as elastic as other trees, so it falls off when the tree is growing. I guess you could say sycamores are more transparent about their growth.

The big sycamore tree in our front yard, though beautiful, always seemed to be in transition. Just like me. As I took tentative, shaky steps in following God through the healing process, I grew. Quickly. Shedding all the things that kept me from him.

ANOTHER SURPRISING TURN

After all that had happened in Fort Worth—the posttraumatic stress, revealing my brokenness to my friends, and the forgiveness ambush—I pretty much figured God had finished healing me. I mean, what else could he ask of me?

Sure, we followed God to Austin to start a church with no stable source of income, no insurance, and three kids under the age of six. But I wasn't afraid of that. It proved to be a ginormous step of faith that strangely didn't scare me. The stuff that still scared me—the stuff where I had to walk closely with Jesus or completely bail to fear—was the random stuff. Like resisting double- and triple-checking the locks on the doors. Or sending my kids off to a brand-new school. Or letting my kids spend the night at a friend's house. The everyday things always scared me more than the big faith moves. For me, the littlest things triggered my old fear response. I never knew when anxiety would surface. I never knew when I would stare fear full in the face.

One day shortly after moving into our house, Emily and I were out running errands. We drove over to the grocery store just blocks from our house. I loaded her in the front part of the grocery cart facing me. She chattered away about which kind of cereal she wanted, like four-year-olds tend to do. Listening to her little voice and checking the cereal prices, I heard another voice, deep in contrast to Emily's.

"Hi, Susie. How are you doing?"

I looked up from the Cocoa Puffs and Rice Krispies to see John from junior high. John . . . the murderer . . . the shooter . . . my neighbor. I startled internally. I hadn't seen him since the day he walked out of the room after killing Mr. Grayson fifteen years earlier.

"Hi, John," I said and instinctively hugged Emily closer.

We stood there in the cereal aisle talking about Austin. My church. His job. The kind of stuff you'd talk about to an old friend. On the outside I looked completely unfazed—all smiley and cheery—as if nothing had ever stood between us.

On the inside I wanted to grab Emily and hide. I wanted to scream at the top of my lungs, *There is a murderer in the grocery store! Run! Run! Run!!!* But of course, I didn't. I stood there— totally, completely, 100 percent afraid—and talked to him.

When John turned and walked away, I hurried out of the grocery store, trembling. I got Emily into the car as fast as I could, and then I plopped in the front seat and cried. A scared, grateful kind of cry. Scared of what had just happened but grateful nothing had just happened.

As I sat there, I remembered my forgiveness ambush—

how John and I were truly on the same team. That made me cry even harder. I still wanted to distance myself from him, but I thought about all the years I had been acting like the prodigal's older brother, sitting in judgment over John. So, crying, I prayed. I asked God to help me with my arrogance. I asked God to continue to seal my forgiveness toward John. And then I asked God to swoop in and speak to John, because I had no idea where he was in the process with God. I understood that if I needed God so desperately for what I had witnessed, John needed God even more desperately for what he had done.

Suddenly compassion stepped into my soul in a space where fear usually stood guard. I had room for something other than fear. Empathy unexpectedly moved in.

FEAR FINAL

The Bible says that when the wise men saw baby Jesus for the first time, they "fell down, and worshipped him."[1] I think we miss the meaning of the original language. When it says they "fell down," we think of all those Bethlehem nativity scenes carved from olive wood. Or we think of the Christmas story plays we watch in December. Or the church musicals. We think of the wise men or kings on one knee. Looking stately and dignified. Tipping their head to Jesus. That kind of bowing.

Well, the real story is "they prostrated themselves and did him homage."[2] I'm no theologian, but I'd like to unpack this a bit.

Prostrate is lying facedown on the floor. Not kneeling as if you're about to be knighted, but a complete and total humbling. In the case of the kings, it undoubtedly meant lying facedown in the stable muck. Seriously. Laid out completely. Hands in the dung. Soiled robes. Crowns knocked off. Faces to the ground.

That is what it means to worship someone.

Before God healed me, it's exactly what I did for fear. I was facedown on the floor, hands in the dirt, addicted to what-ifs and oh nos. I was completely humbling myself and paying homage. To fear. To the Enemy's lies.

From the time I was fourteen until the time I got to Fort Worth at twenty-six, I was on my knees and face on the floor for fear. I obeyed fear. I trusted fear. I adored fear. I was completely humbled before fear. God help me.

Those twelve years represent a slow fade to complete worship of fear. I loved God. But I worshiped fear. Yes, you can do both. But eventually one has to win out. God wars against fear in the heart of believers. Faith says no to fear.

The day I saw John and sat in my car crying, I had a choice to bow down to fear again or to humble my scared little self before God. The good news is, I bowed down to Jesus with the same sort of abandon as when I asked him to save me at twelve. A yes-no-matter-what kind of prostration.

The healing in Fort Worth was legitimate . . . and real. It was good medicine for my sick heart. But even when God heals, we have a choice to stay well or to slip back into sickness. Sitting in the car crying after seeing John, I realized this for the first time. The options were to push through the hard stuff in wholeness or to slink back to my old fearing ways. Instead of freaking out after seeing John, I cried and bowed right there in the car. Then God's Spirit told me to pray for John. And I prayed. To God. For John. I think of that moment in the car as if it were a final exam in fear. And I think—by God's grace—I passed the final.

I think we get to a point of testing. After God graciously walks us through life's bad things—and after he heals us—he expects us to trust him. He expects us to read his Word, believe it, and act on it. No more listening to fear, lying on the floor, face in the muck. We listen up, ready for the new thing, believing God infused us with the wellness necessary to g-r-o-w.

By looking at my story, maybe you're starting to recognize some of the ways God is asking you to trust him. Or maybe you recognize your own fear finals, the places where God requires a new kind of dependence on him instead of yourself.

Okay, may I have permission to talk a little tough with you? You have only two choices: slink back into all kinds of dysfunction, an ongoing affair with fear, and a life full of excuses, or step into all God asks—a radical path of obedience and a life full of breathtaking adventure.

I meet fear-ers every day, and most of them want to step up, but the excuses get in the way. Either they buy into the cultural norm that fearing is the basis of good parenting or the best business decisions. Or they excuse themselves from obedience because their stories provide a loophole. They hold fast to the lie that they are the grand exception and that Jesus couldn't ask for a fearless kind of faith.

Friends, when Jesus said, "Fear not," he didn't leave room for any cultural norms or excuses. As a matter of fact, if anyone ever had a valid exemption, it was Jesus. And you know what he did. He marched forward on the most radical path of obedience possible with these words on his lips: "Father, if you are willing, take this cup from me; yet not my will, but yours be done."[3]

Created by God to do the hard things, to trust in the darkest places, and not only to live to tell about it but also to praise because of it—this is who we are in Christ.

A DIFFERENT SPIRIT

This journey from fear to faith repeats continually in Scripture. God asked the Israelites to step out of fear and into faith all the time. When Moses got the incredible assignment to lead the Israelites out of Egypt, they faced many fear obstacles. Moses led the people forcefully, busting through one fear final after another until finally the people lost courage.

Here's how the story goes. At God's request Moses sent out the leaders of each family to spy on the land of Canaan and give a report.[4] They went, spied, and returned to Moses with this news:

> We went in to the land where you sent us; and it certainly does flow with milk and honey, and this is its fruit. Nevertheless, the people who live in the land are strong, and the cities are fortified and very large; and moreover, we saw the descendants of Anak there. Amalek is living in the land of the Negev and the Hittites and the Jebusites and the Amorites are living in the hill country, and the Canaanites are living by the sea and by the side of the Jordan.[5]

There, standing on the very edge of the Promised Land, the leaders lost courage. After years of oppression from the Egyptians and wandering in the desert, they lost the energy to fight another battle. But there was an exception: Caleb. The Bible describes Caleb as having a "different spirit."[6] Instead of caving to fear while spying on the land, Caleb proclaimed they should take possession of the land and overcome their enemies.[7] In the face of overwhelming odds and a lack of support, Caleb stood prepared to fight the next battle, ready to kick the enemy's butt. What was it about Caleb? How did he stand alone while the rest of the spies lost hope? Another translation of the Bible, the New International Version, gives us a better understanding of Caleb's heart condition when it says that Caleb followed God wholeheartedly.[8] Wholeheartedly, meaning "an undivided heart."

The mystery behind the courageous faithful is not fearlessness but wholeheartedness. A belief that God will come through. It's not about diminishing the giants as much as it is about adoring God with your whole heart. Not so much forgetting the fear as reflecting on the character of your Father. No doubt Caleb's heart fluttered a beat or two as he peered over the edge at the enemy, but he didn't stay focused there. Instead, he threw his heart back up to God. Caleb's love for God overcame his fear.

Another interesting piece of this story is that God rewarded Caleb's wholeheartedness. Conversely, the cowardly crowd suffered for their unfaithfulness via their own children.[9] I don't know about you, but I can't think of a better motivation to try faith instead of fear. I do not want my kids or grandkids to suffer because I was too afraid. Or because my heart waned when my devotion split apart in the face of scary things.

I bet you feel the same way. You'd do anything to keep your kids from suffering for your mistakes. Anything to avoid leaving a legacy of apathetic spirituality. Then you and I must step up and "Calebize" our hearts by following hard after God, praying to love him more every day, and desiring to do what he asks. Sometimes we do this willingly—sometimes not—but always doing it, keeping in step with the next request.

I've heard a quote attributed to Elisabeth Elliot that really sticks with me when I fight the fear battle, and I think it's what Caleb understood: "Sometimes when we are called to obey, the fear does not subside and we are expected to move against the fear. One must choose to do it afraid."

I have learned to follow Jesus afraid. I have learned to do things that frighten me over and over again. I have learned to do life afraid. I know if God can do this with my ridiculously divided heart, it's more than a possibility for you.

IMAGINATION

I hear your questions. How do I love God enough to trust him? How do I actually step up and do the hard things he asks of me? What happens when I feel the fear crowd in around me and I can barely breathe, much less make a smart decision?

The apostle Paul addressed this in 2 Corinthians 10:5 when he said, "Take every thought captive. Casting down imaginations. Bring into captivity every thought to the obedience of Christ."[10]

Instead of all the what-ifs and oh nos while Caleb was spying on the giants, I imagine he cast down imaginations set against wholehearted devotion to God.

So many of the giants I face are in my head. Fear whispers unspeakable things, and I flinch. It whispers the worst-case scenario about my husband, my kids, my mom, or my dad. If my daughter is driving on the highway late at night, fear says, *A flat tire, no cell phone, a criminal sees her and stops* . . . You know the drill. This is when it's time for me to take captive, cast down, and throw those thoughts in prison. And I do that by worshiping Jesus. Just as the wise men worshiped Jesus, I lay prostrate before God and not before my fears.

The minute I sense the battle, I say no to the Enemy and surrender to God.

A lot of times when I'm driving and my eyes happily wander over the gloriousness of Austin, I'll be presented with an opportunity to pick up those "spiritual weapons"[11] and fight. I distinctly remember driving along one day, enjoying my ride, when I had a random thought that my youngest was in danger. My mind was ever widening to the thought—and the horror— and then I said out loud, "No." The thought invaded my mind again, charging in, and again I spoke out loud in the car, "No!" I followed with this prayer:

Thank you, God, for taking care of Sara. Thank you for your protection over her. You are good and kind and constantly watching over her. I love you.

Then I moved my mind back to enjoying the sunny weather.

This is something I do all the time. This is the battle I fight all the time. And I have trained my mind to reject things that are not happening. I knock down the suggestions, the what-ifs, and the lies that something bad is happening when nothing is happening at all.

When the Bible says to "demolish arguments and every pretension that sets itself up against the knowledge of God,"[12] that means you literally attack that sort of stuff that slips into your mind. You have to fight it or it takes you. And you become a freak. I know. I was exhibit A.

We are not made to be captive to the sort of crap the Enemy throws our direction. And it is crap, make no mistake. We're to be about the business of shielding ourselves from it by transforming the way we think. By stepping up to a supernatural kind of thinking and living—the kind of thinking that pleases God, the kind of action God rewards. Although it's hard, it's a much more beautiful way to do life.

Maybe you are tired of fighting those nasty demons. Yes, I get it. It seems our lives here are made up of fighting. But God is gracious. And God is kind. There are resting spots. Shauna Niequist calls them "thin places":

> Thin places: places where the boundary between the divine world and the human world becomes almost nonexistent, and the two, divine and human, can for a moment, dance together uninterrupted. When we find a thin place, anytime, anywhere, we should live differently in the face of it, because if we don't, we miss one of the best moments that life with God has to offer us. These thin places are gifts, treasures, and they're worth changing our lives for.[13]

10

The Burn

S tarting a new church is exhausting. We were always on call, every little minute, every single day. So each summer we made it a priority to get away as a family—and far enough away that we couldn't be called back to town except for an emergency. Our respite during those early years of building Austin Christian Fellowship—and even now—is our family cabin, the Homestead, in Estes Park.

I've always loved Colorado but felt pretty ambivalent about hiking. Will, on the other hand, hikes fanatically. He grew up hiking with his dad, and his love of it lives deep in his soul. Most summers I'd stay at the cabin with our three small children—who were too young to hike—while Will headed to the mountains. But this got old. Fast. So during one trip to the mountains, I finally figured out I had two choices: stay home another day with the kids in the cabin while Will hiked all day, or sign up through the YMCA for a hike and go myself while Will cared for the kids. So I got in the car and headed over to the Sweet Memorial Building and wrote my name on the list to go on a hike the next morning.

I signed up to hike to Ouzel Falls, which is in a more remote section of Rocky Mountain National Park than the majority of the day hikes. The description sounded easy enough: slight elevation gain and just under six miles round trip. A nice, long walk in the woods.

Bright and early the next morning I met with the other folks who had signed up at Sweet Memorial. We climbed into our cars, some of us sharing rides, and drove over to the Wild Basin Trailhead. When we got to the trailhead parking lot, we grabbed a sip of water, tightened our hiking boots, and started up the trail. There were about twenty of us. Families mostly. A few couples. And me.

The path was easy. We were all following our hike master, going in the same direction and seeing all the same things: leaf-scattered paths, small singing creeks, happy birds, and scampering chipmunks. I fell in rhythm walking alongside a twelve-year-old girl. I asked her about her hometown and how she liked school. Engrossed in conversation, I failed to notice much going on around me except when the hike master stopped to tell us things about the forest.

Every half mile or so he turned to address the group with interesting details. He described the differences between a lodge pole pine, a spruce, and a fir. He pointed out delicate flora: yarrow, buttercup, and columbine. He showed us the difference between bear and elk scratches on an aspen tree.

He pointed out tall things and small things. We walked and walked, putting the miles behind us. Then, when we were about halfway to the top, the hike master stopped walking and started talking about the Ouzel fire. We were no longer in the shadows of the dense forest; instead, we were standing in bright sunlight. I squinted toward the sun that was suspended in the sky, then looked down all around me.

Everywhere I looked I witnessed evidence of a forest fire. Charred, fallen pine trees. Scorched groves of aspen standing still like wooden soldiers against the pale-blue sky. As far as I could see in every direction was evidence of devastation. Like walking through an expansive battlefield, a graveyard of trees.

While just minutes earlier I stood sheltered in the shadow of a pristine forest, I now stood exposed to a graphic landscape. Full of fatalities. Hundreds and hundreds of acres of death. I reached down to touch a fallen tree. Ash blacked my fingertips. Was the fire just yesterday?

When I looked back up, as sure as I have ever heard God in

my life, I heard him whisper, *This is your soul. You experienced a burn.*

I stood, stunned, my eyes wandering from one dead tree to another. At first I felt confused. My soul a burn? I couldn't piece the picture together. Then in a flash I understood. Yes, I had experienced a burn in my life. That day in May of 1978 when I witnessed the murder, a fire ignited in my soul. It created a burn. I felt the fire that made me doubt God. It made me wonder if he was trustworthy and made me question his character and his love. Yes, I'd had a burn in my life.

If I could have reached inward and touched my soul, black ash would have marked my hand.

I gaped at the huge blue sky and thousand-acre burn. A very small me standing on a trail with a very, very big God. And he was everywhere. Like Isaiah when he saw a revelation upon the death of his cousin, Uzziah, the king of Judah, I was standing on holy ground. The "train of his robe"[1] filled the mountainside.

As far as I could see, it was as if I were looking at a huge natural mirror of my life. The charred mountainside a physical representation of my soul. God looking down on me, wrapping me up in revelation. Much like the Mozart moment but this time in place of pain, beauty.

I looked around, utterly ambushed by the splendor, as if heaven had peeked out from behind the sky and spilled all over the mountains. And as I stood there in the middle of this gigantic revelation, I realized God had just delivered the deepest, most personal love note on the side of the devastated mountain. I started crying as God's love absolutely overwhelmed me. He was so real to me I felt he was literally standing beside me.

The hike master started talking. The group started moving. But I stood longer—in quiet reverence. Understanding this truth: God sees me. He is here. And he walks with me in my grief, in my pain, in my recovery.

My feet started moving. I followed along, but my eyes kept me preoccupied. It seemed that for every charred, fallen tree, something green grew underneath. For every bit of blackened death, life. Little bits of new growth sprang up under the dead things. Tiny yellow flowers. Delicate ferns hidden beneath fallen logs. And then I noticed all the small, green saplings realizing a second chance at life. Scraggly, tender little trees, like the cottonwood my dad planted, but this time they grew everywhere. As far as I could see, baby trees reached up toward the sun. There in front of my eyes, I saw "the smallest hope."[2] I saw evidence that God takes even the bad things and makes something new. And lovely.

New revelation. Fresh tears. And a gentle but determined confession to God: *You are good. You are kind. You are trustworthy. You are holy. Oh, thank you for loving me. For caring for me. For showing me the smallest hope.*

On that forest trail God presented a truth too big to contain, a love story too generous to deny. Because I understood—as if for the first time—how very personal my pain was to God. And how very personal his love is for me. After all he did to heal me in Fort Worth, and now this? A beautiful, giant picture of his redemptive love, reminding me that he can be trusted in all things because his love for me stands strong enough to accompany my soul through the burn and plant hope on the other side.

The rest of the hike I was a mess. I got up the mountain. I got down. But the entire time I cried, constantly wiping tears away as they fell underneath my sunglasses. I thought the story was done. How could God make himself any more clear about his love and his care? How could he possibly be more obvious?

SONS AND DAUGHTERS

Why does God want to heal us? Why does he care to use a forest burn to embrace his daughter and kiss her on the cheek? Does it make you wonder? The burn made me wonder. But when I rediscovered a woman in the New Testament who wanted healing from a hemorrhage, I started to understand more.

Twelve straight years of bleeding, seeing doctors, doing anything and everything she could to get well. Then finally,

Jesus comes to town. And she thinks, *If I can just touch his robe, I'll be healed.*

So she does something very brave. She manages to push through the crowd to get close to Jesus. She reaches out quietly, secretively, to touch the edge of his cloak. It happens. She is healed. Instantly!

But then something unexpected . . . Jesus turns around. He asks out loud, "Who touched me?"

The disciples shake their heads and try to get him to back off the question and move on. There are so many people—how could they ever determine who touched him? The crowd jostles restlessly. But he waits. And waits. Letting the tension build.

Imagine the poor woman, hiding in the crowd. Pushed tight against those listening, fear silencing her as Jesus asks again, "Who touched me?"

I've always wondered, why did Jesus ask who touched him? Why the tension? Don't you think he knew who touched him? And even if he didn't know, why would he create certain anxiety for her, persisting in asking and waiting?

Without exception, when I ask this question, people answer the same sort of things:

Because Jesus wanted to make her an example.
Because he wanted the crowd to see the story of
how he healed her.

Because he wanted to use her life as an example
to the glory of God.

Well, I don't know.

I mean, I don't think God sets up his kids to suffer just so he can set them on a platter of observation for others. God is not detached from our suffering. He does not seek public glory through our private pain. This whole idea of suffering solely for God so he can get something out of it makes him so unfatherly, doesn't it? As if God can't get what he wants without making our stories climactic for himself—at our expense. Like a puppet master toying with us. No.

I think Jesus turned around because he loved her. He wanted to see her. To hold her face and look in her eyes. I think Jesus wanted to spend time connecting with her because he loved her and wanted to bless her, not because he wanted to make a spectacle of her for his glory.

Jesus has all the glory he needs without our help. God doesn't need us. But as evidenced here in the story, he wants us. He wants to be with us, near to us. And he'll go to any extent to stop us, look us in the eye, and hold our faces in his hands. This is Jesus. The only One able to heal us and free us from our fears.

He calls us son or daughter, just as he did the woman in this story. He heals us and he sends us in peace. Free from the fear affliction.

I don't know where you are in your struggle to trust God. But I do know this: God's whole aim for you is reconciliation and intimacy with him. I don't think God finds pleasure in your suffering or your pain or your anxiety. That's not the nature of a good father.

THE NATURE OF A GOOD FATHER

My dad just celebrated his eighty-first birthday. But you'd never know it. It doesn't stop him from heading out in his white pickup truck to his ranch at Cow Creek and digging big holes with his shovel, then plopping a new tree in the ground. His age doesn't keep him from dragging a water hose all around the fifty-acre property to make sure his new trees get a good, long drink in the hot summer months. To me, my dad seems ageless. But he's not, of course.

His recent knee-replacement surgery reminded me of just how long he's been alive. Honestly, seeing him in his hospital gown, working with the physical therapist to walk a very few steps down the hall, nearly killed me, because I think of my dad as invincible. In my mind he can do anything, even at eighty-one. And I know there's nothing he wouldn't do for me. Even now.

My dad loves me. Lavishly. He provides for me, just as he does for my sister and brother. Sharing his hard-earned resources.

Every once in a while a check will arrive in a white envelope. Or he'll tuck a twenty-dollar bill in my hand to "pay" for the bread I made him.

My dad feels protective of us—and he's not afraid to show it. Though Bob Gerrie may be the friendliest man you'll ever meet, don't test him by being unkind to his kids or grandkids. Because then he's a papa bear. Grizzly type.

My dad wants to be with us on special occasions and no-big-deal kinds of days. Whether we grab a hamburger at Top Notch or all meet at my parents' house for Thanksgiving dinner, time spent together makes him happy because he loves us so much.

For as long as I can remember, my dad played the role of comforter. He carries these soft, white cotton handkerchiefs with him at all times. And if ever he sees tears coming, he'll whip out a handkerchief and hand it to me. I'll dry my tears as we talk. Then we share a big hug, and every single time he says, "I love you. I'm so proud of you."

I have a whole drawer full of my dad's white handkerchiefs, like love notes to me. He's a good man who loves God . . . and loves me.

I know by now that not everyone gets a chance to have a dad like that. Someone who provides, protects, and comforts. Not everyone gets a big hug or an "I love you" from a father. Maybe you never heard your dad say, "I'm so proud of you." It's something I don't understand. And it's something that seems truly unfair. If this is your story, I wish I could reach through the page and hand you a white handkerchief.

I don't know where you are with your dad. But I want you to know God loves you. God is a good father. A kind father. And a wise father who gives good gifts.[4] The Bible says in God "the fatherless find compassion."[5]

God is the *perfect* Father. Completely holy. He's there for you when you're angry, defiant, and ripped up over life. His love for you doesn't change. No matter what has happened in the past or what will happen in the future, your heavenly Father loves you. He willingly moves mountains for you. Or in my case, burns them up. Because that's how the Father loves.

ONE MILLION DOLLARS

Two years ago I found myself sitting in a circle at a writers conference when a facilitator posed this question: What would you do if you woke up tomorrow with one million dollars?

These writers offered the most amazing ideas. Things like paying off their parents' house or moving to Uganda to build shelters for orphans. Big things.

Honestly, the first thing I thought was how nice it would be to pay off college for our three kids. Or build a house with a view. But then I realized we don't need a view. And Will and I enjoy working. Doing ministry. So while paying off college would be nice, it probably isn't something I'd choose to do with a million dollars. We'll get there one day.

I listened as my writer friends talked about these incredible ideas and generous contributions. Around the circle they went. So I decided to think deep and crazy and wide with my million.

And then I thought about you.

Suddenly, with all certainty, I realized what I'd do with my million dollars tomorrow morning. I'd fly you to Colorado so you and I could hike up to Ouzel Falls, so you and I could hike through the burn.

As a matter of fact, since a million bucks would cover more than just you and me, it might be nice if you'd invite a few friends. We'd all fly into Denver, head over the ridge to the sleepy, sweet town of Estes Park, and pick up some comfortable sturdy boots for our hike.

Then we'd all stay at Wind River, because the people at Wind River are so nice. They're like family. But also because it's just a couple of miles from the Ouzel Falls trailhead, where God spoke to me through the burn.

We'd eat a home-cooked supper and laugh and get to know one another better. We'd listen to each other's stories. Thoughtfully . . . the way a father listens when his child is having trouble at school. Tenderly . . . the way a mother listens when a child feels wounded by a best friend.

After dinner we'd all walk quietly to our cabins in the cold night under a big, black sky dotted by a million tiny stars and the faint shadow of Longs Peak ahead. A promise full of hope, because God speaks quiet and true in the mountains. Every time.

And the next day we'd get up early and hike the burn together. I'd take you up that same leaf-scattered path and then on to the scarred landscape. I'd show you the acres and acres of mountain war zone. I'd have you reach down, touch a fallen pine, and then marvel at the ash on your hand. Ash—still present after all this time. How long has it been? It looks like yesterday. Then I'd ask if the burn reminded you of your soul too.

That's what I'd do with a million dollars. Because I want you to know the love of God as Father. I want you to understand the lengths he'll go to . . . just for you.

THE BURN

I didn't tell you one very important thing: what happened one week after I hiked Ouzel Falls for the first time, the day God revealed the burn.

When I got back home to Austin, I was still thinking about the burn. Curious about all the details of the fire—wondering if knowing more would piece together the big picture for me—I decided to find out more about it. I sat on my bed and made a phone call to the Rocky Mountain National Park ranger station.

I learned a lot about the fire. The park ranger explained that the fire started because of lightning. He told me since it was ignited by natural causes, the fire was allowed to burn, creating an organic cleanse for the forest. But after burning for more than a month and getting way out of control, more than five hundred firefighters were called in to put out the fire. In all, more than a thousand acres burned in the Ouzel fire, making it the largest fire to date in the park.

This was amazing information. But nothing could prepare me for the one detail I wasn't expecting. I asked the ranger when the fire had occurred, and I couldn't even speak when I heard his answer.

The fire took place in 1978.

The very same year I witnessed the murder.

I sat on the edge of the bed, stunned. After a moment I found my voice and thanked him for the information. I hung up the phone, crumbled off the bed, and sat weeping on the floor. Completely overwhelmed at my Father's tender mercies.

REGENERATION

The burn made such an indelible impact on me. The more I thought about everything I had seen, the more of a marvel it became in my life. Will wanted to experience it too, so the following summer we hiked the burn together.

We took our time. Walked it slowly, listening for God and snapping pictures along the way. At a certain bend along the trail, we found a tiny pine tree—not more than two feet tall—growing behind the base of a charred, fallen tree. A complete wonder. This beautiful, delicate tree sprang up from beneath obvious trauma. Will named the tree Sparky.

That tiny tree came to epitomize the whole, big thing God did for me. A little living love note, standing there tender and green. A tiny tree slowly reaching upward out of the ash of the past. Cute little Sparky.

That small tree standing bravely on the scorched mountainside is a constant reminder to me of how God brings life out of death. A little, living Ebenezer. Reminding me God is holy, holy, holy, and no matter how dark things look, "the whole earth is full of his glory."[6]

Somewhere, somehow God is leaving you love notes too. Reminders that he hasn't left you, won't leave you, and isn't done telling your whole story.

11

Finally at Home

I answered the phone. I instantly recognized his voice, but he sounded different somehow, worried and even sad. I listened intently, wishing he would get his words out quickly, because I didn't know what in the world he needed to say on the other end of the phone.

Susie . . . they cut down our cottonwood. I was just driving by Murchison, and I saw the city work crews out there. They were cutting down our tree. I couldn't believe it. They told me the tree wasn't structurally sound so they were forced to remove it as a safety issue. Worried it would tumble over unexpectedly and possibly hurt the kids. I stood there and watched as they cut it down. There was nothing I could do . . . but I asked them if

I could have what was left of the trunk. I have it here in the back of my pickup.

This is my dad. Stopping everything to save a tree. And just for me. Salvaging whatever he could get of the cottonwood we watered together at the school when I was just a child.

I drove over to his house immediately. When I pulled up in the driveway, I saw my then-seventy-year-old dad unloading massive pieces of the cottonwood tree into the yard. When I got out of the car, I went straight to my dad and gave him a big hug. I listened as he told me he was sorry, because he knew the tree meant so much to me. He knew how the presence of the tree at the junior high represented such a big part of God's story to me. How it distracted me from the memory of the murder because the tree obstructed my view of the window and the room where the murder took place. And how the tree overshadowed the bad memory with the good memory of our watering the little tree.

I listened, in tears. But then I told him the bigger story that remains: I have a dad who loves me and would stop everything to pick up pieces of a cottonwood trunk and bring them home for me. And even more amazing, I have a heavenly Father who loves me. Because God had my dad intentionally plant the tree years before we even knew what would happen that day in May of 1978.

Nothing can kill that kind of love. No bad thing will ever outdo God's goodness. Is it any wonder I understand the Father's love? And see love notes floating down like leaves from a tree? That tree—and all the trees in my life, really—are love notes God left for me. Planned out years in advance while he waited patiently for me to have eyes that see.[1]

A BEAUTIFUL THING

Of all the stories in the Bible, this one may convict me the most. Jesus and his disciples meet at the house of a guy named Simon. They walk into the house and sit at this big table. I don't know what they were talking about. Maybe how Jesus healed Simon of leprosy. Or maybe they were trying to unpack the things Jesus said about his death. Whatever the conversation was that evening, in the middle of this dinner together, a woman walks in. Her name is Mary.[2]

The Bible says Mary was "a certain immoral woman."[3] That's a nice way of saying Mary was a prostitute. A harlot. A whore. A woman who gave herself—and gave sex—to men who were not her husband.

So this Mary enters the room where all these men sit with Jesus. They look at her. Probably scornfully. Maybe even lustfully. She feels the tension, fully aware of their judgment. But instead of being intimidated or scared away by their judgment, she does something uncustomary. She kneels down by Jesus, breaks open an alabaster box full of expensive perfume, and pours it all over his feet. She cries while she's doing this, weeping, the Bible says, and uses her hair to wipe the tears off his feet.

The men at the table are very uncomfortable. They are even indignant—over the reputation of the woman, over the show of affection, and even over the expensive perfume "wasted" on Jesus. But Jesus defends her, this weeping mess at his feet. He defends the broken woman and the broken box, saying, "She has done a beautiful thing to me."

I don't know about you, but I want to do a beautiful thing for Jesus. And I want my life to be a beautiful thing for Jesus. I want him to see me and my life and then say, "She has done a beautiful thing to me."

But I have realized something. That won't happen if I hold on to fear. Because fear is not beautiful—it is dark and ugly. An oppressive master. A gruesome monster. The lure of safety ends in unfaithfulness to God.

When I give myself over to the what-ifs and oh nos, I am a whore for worry. A harlot for fear. So I must do something brave and uncustomary. I must live my life without these big, forceful ideas of culture that say, "Be safe. Be careful." And I must break open the box of my perceived safety and spill it all over Christ's feet. Emptying all I am and all I hold dear to God alone.

I have realized with all certainty that it means I must daily walk away from fear. And the only way I can hope to do that is to think of fear the same way my Father thinks of fear. As an idol in my life.

Fear is an idol that robs me of believing God can manage my life without my help.

An idol that emasculates my view of God, stripping him of his dignity and sovereignty.

An idol that separates me from intimacy with God.

The truth is, unless I think of fear the same way my Father thinks of fear, I will never feel safe. And so I will never truly be home with God or be able to trust him.

As you read this, maybe you feel the urge to let go and fall at Jesus's feet, but fear pimped you, leaving you feeling ugly and ashamed. I know. Better yet, Jesus already knows. And he doesn't care what condition you find yourself in. He still wants you. All of you.

And, yes, you can do something beautiful for Christ. Because he welcomes the fear-ers, the fail-ers, all of us.

LAUGH AT THE FUTURE

People who knew me then and know me now wonder at the "how" behind my transformation. How did I go from a complete fear freak to a confident person? Honestly, it's hard even for me to understand. And you need to know, it wasn't an overnight miracle, believe me. The best person to ask would be the one who has lived through it all with me.

He had no idea what a mess of a woman he married twenty-plus years ago. I was all shiny and Jesus-y on the outside. But on the inside? Wow. What a mess. My heart needed repair. The kind of fixing that Will couldn't do. The mending of stuff he couldn't touch.

A couple of months after I fell apart, in what I call the Fort Worth phase, Will became acutely aware of the depth of my fear issues, and he started praying something specific regarding my fear stronghold. Will started praying these two things straight from Scripture:

> He prayed I would be clothed with strength
> > and dignity.
> And he prayed I would laugh without fear of
> > the future.[4]

He didn't tell me what he was praying; he just prayed. Every day. He prayed I would be clothed with strength and dignity when I was too scared to stay overnight without him. He prayed I would laugh without fear of the future when I was freaked out about the details of parenting—like where to send our kids to school and whether they should go to a sleepover. He prayed.

I imagine God moved me down the line as fast as I could manage, which ended up being a five- to ten-year process. So, yes, I was a s-l-o-w learner. Examining every tentative step I took. Looking to God for confirmation. Affirmation. But I did go from a terrified, worrisome woman to a confident one. I went from someone always expecting the worst to someone looking for the best. A "good news" kind of person.

I actually was so changed by God's Spirit and Will's prayers that I became a zealot for good news. It wasn't enough that my life was changed; I wanted to help others change theirs too. Through any avenue I could, I talked to people about how God changed my life. I went from being protective, even paranoid, about discussing the details of my life to being completely open. I spoke and wrote regularly about how God changed me. I encouraged others to have faith instead of fear. This is the kind of thing God does with former fear-ers. He turns their lives inside out.

No doubt it would be much easier to sit safe and quiet with all God did for me. To revel in this miracle privately instead of letting you see all my weirdness and weakness. But you must know . . . I don't want you to feel alone. And I desperately want you to realize God can change things. He can make you new. He can turn your whole life around.

FULL-CIRCLE REDEMPTION

My dear friend Kristin has a huge, gorgeous, mature magnolia tree in her front yard. Every time I walk past it going to her front door, I wonder at God's creativity and his way of bringing closure and redemption to a story.

Kristin and I met through social media. We had mutual friends, lived in the same neighborhood, and liked the same kinds of things. So I guess it was just a matter of time before we became good friends. At some point in time, we should have bumped into each other at the grocery store or something, but that never happened. What did happen was that I contacted her and talked her into attending a writers conference in San Diego with me.

When I told my mom about my upcoming trip and my new friend, she mentioned that Kristin lived just up the street from her. How interesting . . . Kristin and my mom, neighbors.

The date for the conference came. Kristin and I flew out together, shared a room, and had an absolute ball. By the weekend's finish, we concluded we should collaborate on a writing/cooking project we'd call *52 Sunday Suppers*. When we got back to Austin, we planned to have our first meeting at her house.

I'll never forget the first time I walked into her lovely house and sat down at her dining room table. I looked up at her and smiled, confessing I never in a million years thought I would end up inside *that* house—the very house I was scared even to drive or jog by when I was in high school. The house that was the home to the boy who killed my teacher—and was now the home to my new friend, Kristin. But here I was, having tea in her beautiful home. And here I was, sitting at the table, praying with Kristin over our plans to reach out to moms and encourage them to sit down at the table together with their families and friends over dinner.

I was completely comfortable at Kristin's house. There was no fear. No weird feelings. No worries. Things do change. God is always at work making the saddest or scariest parts of our story beautiful. He is always undoing the things the Enemy has done to us—and turning them into good. Something far beyond our wildest imagination.

But God didn't stop there. Nope. He worked out the details to do something even more stunning to the place I never wanted to set foot in after that day in May 1978. The place where the bad thing happened.

Our church, Austin Christian Fellowship, makes its home about fifteen minutes from our house in a neighborhood west of town. We've had that great location for more than ten years. But about two years ago, we started feeling God's direction to take the church out to other neighborhoods, to make the church more accessible for people so they could be a church community in the community in which they live.

Our second community church ended up being in our own neighborhood, led by a great guy named Thom Fulmer. Thom went right to work trying to find a location for what we call ACF Northwest—or ACFnw.

Would it surprise you to find out Thom decided Murchison Junior High was the perfect place for the church? Yes. A church—our church—landed in the very place where the bad thing happened. Ironic? No. That's God. That's God saying, *I'm not done here yet. This ending has my name on it.*

I remember the first day ACFnw met in Murchison. I went to celebrate and support. When I walked in the front door, I was greeted by people I love. People who love God.

There was Kyle, whom I've known since elementary school and was at Murchison when the murder took place, holding open the door and giving me a big ol' hug. There was Sandra, who has been at ACF since its inception, smiling and handing out programs. There were my parents, greeting people and laughing. And there were lots of people I didn't know, people coming to our new little church. People hungry for God.

This was *nothing* like the last time I was in Murchison Junior High.

I especially wanted to go to ACFnw that day because my oldest daughter, Emily, had been hired months earlier at ACFnw to lead the student ministry. Yes, more God.

When Emily described where the students would meet, I realized it was the old choir room they used in 1978 to give group counseling after the murder. Fast-forward twenty-plus years, and it's the room where my daughter stands, telling kids about Jesus.

And the courtyard Cheryle and I ran through screaming way back in 1978? It's the courtyard where my daughter Sara plays her guitar and sings Hillsong United's "Oceans" while my daughter Emily baptizes kids who love Jesus.

The cafeteria where I took the test to determine whether I would be in the gifted and talented program at Murchison—the test that placed me in the classroom with all the other students who witnessed the murder—is now the place I lift up my hands and sing to God. With my neighbors and friends, I sing, "Holy, holy, holy."

Good news triumphs bad news.

This is God at work. Full circle. This is the kind of thing that makes me know he is in control, that he's always been in control. Stuff that no person could arrange. No human could make my ending so beautiful and so personal. No one but God.

God is in the business of fulfillment. God keeps the promises he makes. He made big promises to Abraham—and he kept them.[5] He made colossal promises to Moses—and he kept them.[6] He made a huge promise to David, which he kept.[7] And aren't we grateful for that promise? Because his name is Jesus.

And he's made promises to you too.

When God makes a promise, you can count on him to keep it. When he says you will see goodness in the land of the living,[8] believe it. When he says he is a strong protector and completely trustworthy in every situation,[9] you can count on it.

I don't know what kind of hopelessness you face because of fear, but I know God has a promise for you, and because of that, you can live unafraid in an unsafe world.

Expect God to be bigger than your worst nightmare, and know him as Immanuel,[10] God with you.

HOME

For so many years I wondered about my safety and my security. I felt as though I had to create a safe place for my kids and my husband—and all the other people I loved. I thought it was my job to be in charge of caring for them. It left me tired—achingly tired—and always longing for rest and comfort.

All those years I spent running my own life, I was running away from God. It was when I finally broke apart and accepted my neediness before God that I realized comfort. When I let go—because I literally had to—I finally got well. And then, at the end of it all, there was God. Right where he had always been. Ready to offer the comfort I craved. The security I longed for. The home I always wanted.

In the Old Testament, Moses called God "home." He said, "Lord, through all the generations you have been our home!"[11] God was their dwelling place, their refuge, their place of safety. With all those years of wandering under his belt, Moses acknowledged that God is home.

Like those Israelites I've done my share of wandering. I spent more than a decade looking for comfort in control and safety. It was only when I finally released my fears that I found home, just like Moses. It was God I was seeking all along. He is the God of answered prayers and perfected endings.

God is home.

Epilogue

Because of a Tree

In my backyard grows an enormous bur oak. It stands over forty feet tall, with large green leaves shading half our yard. My dad planted it there as a sapling years ago. But before the tree stood as even a two-foot tall, scraggly Charlie Brown tree, it was a seed. An acorn. Just an inconsequential little something that would easily fit in the palm of your hand.

The bur oak in my backyard didn't magically end up there. My dad made a plan for it. He wanted to gift the tree to my family and me, so years before the tree was even big enough to plant in the ground, he went to work. He headed down to Hyde Park Baptist Church, our home church while I was growing up in Austin, and gathered six big, healthy-looking acorns from underneath the massive hundred-year-old bur oak across from the sanctuary. Then he took those acorns to his house and placed them in six small clay pots full of potting soil.

Because he knew the squirrels in his backyard would want to dig up those tasty acorns and eat them, he put chicken wire across the tops of the pots to protect the acorns. Then he watered them and waited. Watered and waited. About three months later several of the acorns became tiny saplings.

He nurtured the saplings, watching them carefully while keeping the predators away. And months and months later, when the babies proved ready, he brought one over to my house in a big bucket.

I remember the day well. My dad, my husband, and my son grabbed shovels from the garage; my girls ran around in the backyard. We still had a playscape back then, so the girls climbed to the top to watch while I grabbed my camera to take a few shots. After choosing the perfect spot in the backyard, the guys went to work with the shovels and dug a big hole for the tree. Then my dad positioned the little tree in its new home while explaining how the tree needed lots of deep watering during the first few months. Thirty minutes later the baby bur oak sat sunning in the yard, happily soaking up water from a nearby hose.

I love the bur oak tree. It reminds me of my dad's funny obsession with trees. I also love the tree because it's a physical representation of my father's love and care for my extended family—my dad gifted my sister and brother with bur oak trees in their yards too. But mainly I love that tree because I love my dad. I am overwhelmed at how he's loved me, cared for me, and encouraged me all my life.

Just like my heavenly Father. He's planted trees all over just for me. To show his love, his care, his encouragement. I see God because of those trees.

In the same kinds of ways, God plants hope in your life. It might not be through trees, but I promise you, his love and care are there for you. No matter what you've been through or who you've become because of the heartache or sin in your life, God loves you.

WHERE ARE YOU?

God asks us a question. It's tucked away in the narrative of Adam and Eve in Genesis after they made the bad decision regarding the fruit of the Tree of the Knowledge of Good and Evil.

As the story goes, Eve listens to the serpent. She caves in to the temptation to disbelieve the character of God—that he is always good and kind and watching out for her best interest. She believes the lies of the Evil One, and then she takes the fruit, eats a bite, and hands it to Adam, who does the same.

Immediately upon eating the fruit, Adam and Eve feel embarrassed. Ashamed. Aware of their nakedness. They grab big leaves from the trees and sew clothes to hide their newfound shame. Later, in the cool of the evening when they hear God walking nearby in the garden, they hide from God. God calls out to them, "Where are you?"[1]

I love this part of the story . . . how God is walking in the garden he created, seeking his favorites, who are made in his image, Adam and Eve. How he desires their company. And so he asks them, "Where are you?"

I think he asks us the same question. He wants to be with us—no matter if fear has us cowering under the counter. Or hypercontrolling our children. Or any other result of the presence of fear in our lives. We don't need to dread God or his plans for our lives. We just need to answer honestly where we are in relation to him.

The only way to live unafraid is to be honest with yourself and with God.

Where are you?

HOPE TEND-ERS

Maybe like me, you're just waking up from the biggest fear fake-out of your life. You are looking back, realizing you wasted time, energy, and precious relationships being a fear freak. It's then that you think you're a total loser—naked and ashamed from believing the lies. Wrapped up in leaves of shame. But did you know there is even more good news? Scripture promises:

> There is therefore now no condemnation for those who
> are in Christ Jesus.[2]

God does not accuse you. He is not holding anything against you. As a matter of fact, he's so crazy in love with you, so full of forgiveness toward you, he wants to shower you with blessings until you're soaking wet. He's already filled your life with love notes so you will "grow in the grace and knowledge of Jesus."[3]

We must grow big in faith, not fear. We have to fill up with the good news, not the bad news. It takes some time to go from a position of overwhelming unbelief in God's goodness and holiness to overwhelming belief in his goodness and holiness no matter what. Though staunch fear-ers might think they could never get there, with Christ anything is possible.[4]

I love that Adam's first job in the garden was as a tend-er. "The LORD God placed the man in the Garden of Eden to tend and watch over it."[5] God planted and grew the big, gorgeous garden; Adam was there to cultivate and nurture it. To work in it and guard it. To take care of God's goodness.

I think we're still supposed to be tend-ers. We tend the hope and courage God plants inside our souls when we read what he says to us. When we listen to the Spirit. When we hold fast to the good news.

When we wake up before sunrise and see the sun peeking over the horizon, calling the clouds together all pink and orange and pale blue, we feel bits of hope springing up, surrounding us. When we visit a new mama in the hospital and hold her precious newborn, so small and fresh and snuggly, we feel hope surge inside. When we plant a tiny green sapling in the dark, rich soil and believe it will grow and grow and someday become a big shade tree in our yard, that is hope.

Those kinds of things are easy to identify. And they are easy to see. But they are not the only ways God places hope inside of us. God plants hope in the smallest ways. In the secret places. Love notes.

I don't know how God communicates his love to you. I only know how he communicates his love to me. But I do know he loves all his kids the same, and so I know—because I truly believe what I read in the Bible—that God is always communicating his love to his children.

He's planting seeds of hope in our hearts—that is his job. And it is our job to cultivate the hope.

I think that probably means when you are a fear freak who is too scared to sleep at home alone, you listen for God's voice saying that things will be all right, and you set your head down on your pillow at night agreeing, "He gives sleep to his be-loved."[6] When you wake up the next morning, rested, and get a glimpse of the morning clouds all pink and orange and pale blue, you have tended God's hope inside you.

It means when you become a parent and feel completely stressed out about the responsibility, you agree with God that he is in total control of your child. And you agree with God that he loves your child more than you ever will. And you say yes to God's sovereignty regarding that child every single day.

It means when you see a big ol' tree, its leafy canopy reach-ing toward the heavens, you remember that tree was once a small seed. Inconsequential though it once seemed, it now stands tall by God's grace.

Hope says, *God will give beauty for ashes. Joy instead of mourning. Praise instead of despair.*

Hope says, *We are strong and graceful oaks for his glory.*[7]

FOREST AND THE TREE

For several Septembers in a row, Will and I have had the opportunity to go to Wind River in Estes Park, Colorado, to speak at a couples retreat. But last September, Will led the re-treat without me because of a serious health issue I faced—a whole other story in itself.

Will told me he decided not only to share my story of the

burn and the little tree in the ashes, Sparky, but also to take a group from the retreat and actually hike to Ouzel Falls to show them. He said people really responded to hearing my story and were eager to *see* the story.

He loaded a Suburban full of adults and drove over to the Wild Basin Trailhead. They piled out, tightened their hiking boots, and got a sip of water before they started the six-mile hike. On the trail Will talked with them about the details of the forest and the burn. Around every corner he anticipated showing them the drastic change from densely shaded forest to stark, barren landscape, but something interesting had happened.

Will couldn't believe his eyes when he rounded the corner to see little Sparky, only to find a very large, tall Sparky, who had pushed the dead, ashen stump out of its way. There were still some signs of the burn. The vista was still there—you could still see for miles and miles. But the forest floor was so green and lush that it was hard to find evidence of the burn at all.

I laughed when Will told me the story, because so much of my life mirrors the burn, even now. I don't look at all like the girl hiding under the counter. I'm not the young mom who was frightened her infant would get the flu. No longer the woman scared to stay home alone or fly on an airplane. Not suffering panic attacks and other fear freak-outs.

I'm happy to say I'm more like Sparky—pushing dead

things out of the way to get more light and more space to grow in God's grace.

I'm a former fear-er, publishing his glorious deeds,[8] honestly overwhelmed at how much God has done for me.[9] God is good and does only good.[10] He has done wonderful things! And by his grace I'm going to tell not only my kids but also my grandkids about all the mighty miracles God has done in my life.[11] I'm going to share all these God stories so they can set their hope on God and live unafraid.

And guess what. You can too. By trusting God to do these kinds of things for you, you can live unafraid. We'll be former fear-ers together, you and me.

How amazing are the deeds of the Lord![12]

Discussion Questions

1. What are some of the sources of your biggest fears?

2. How does fear manipulate your behavior?

3. What are the things in your life God could have stopped but didn't?

4. In what ways do you believe fear keeps you safe?

5. How do you take care of your family and yourself "just in case"?

6. How would you answer Jesus's question "Why are you so afraid?"

7. Why is accessing the past often necessary for living unafraid?

8. What strongholds do you see in your past? Are they still reaching into your future?

9. What keeps you from praying the dangerous prayer: *God, if there is anything in me that needs healing, please heal me?*

10. What are some of your "Yet you are holy" moments?

11. I describe myself as having an affair with fear. How would you characterize your relationship with fear?

12. In what ways do you think unforgiveness insulates you from bad things happening?

13. How does fear keep you from doing a beautiful thing for Jesus with your life?

Study Guide

Chapter One: On the Curb

1. How does fear manipulate your behavior?

2. In what ways does fear make you feel safe?

3. What does a fear-er look like? How does he or she act?

4. How does God speak to you most often?

Chapter Two: Promises

1. What are some of the sources of your biggest fears?

2. What do you have trouble trusting God with?

3. In what ways have you experienced a breakup with God?

4. What are the things in your life God could have stopped but didn't?

5. In what ways do you feel God abandoned you?

6. What situations in your life make you wonder why?

Chapter Three: The Losing Team

1. Why does a cut-and-paste theology result in an inauthentic faith?

2. In what ways do you believe fear keeps you safe?

3. What types of fear-induced behavior boss your life around?

4. How did Jesus throw an intercepted pass and lose the game in your life?

5. What kinds of agreements might you be making with the Enemy?

Chapter Four: Easy Prey

1. How do you metaphorically check in the closets or under the beds when it comes to fear?

2. How do you take care of your family and yourself "just in case"?

3. How would you answer Jesus's question "Why are you so afraid?"

4. What are some of your escape routes when you don't feel like trusting God?

Chapter Five: Close to the Cradle

1. What are the dark pieces of your past that might have a hold on you?

2. Why is accessing the past often necessary for living unafraid?

3. What strongholds do you see in your past? Are they still reaching into your future?

4. How would you answer this question if Jesus asked, "Do you want to be made well?"

5. List a few of your Fridays.

Chapter Six: Flat on the Floor

1. Can you think of a time God loved you through the worst thing?

2. What keeps you from praying the dangerous prayer: *God, if there is anything in me that needs healing, please heal me?*

3. What are some of your "Yet you are holy" moments?

4. What is the point of God asking us to acknowledge that he is holy no matter what?

5. How has God put on the brakes in your life to capture your attention and point you to living life unafraid?

6. Where do you most often seek peace?

Chapter Seven: Crying Out Loud

1. What is it about community that scares you?

2. I describe myself as having an affair with fear. How would you characterize your relationship with fear?

3. Everybody has sad, weird, confusing stuff in life. What are some things you have never talked about?

4. How is vulnerability linked to mourning?

5. Why does a lack of mourning end up leaving you anxious and depressed?

6. What has God said to you through community with others?

Chapter Eight: A Big Misunderstanding

1. What kind of irrational things do you think protect you from the bad things in life?

2. In what ways do you think unforgiveness insulates you from bad things happening?

3. How have you misunderstood God's heart in relation to other people or scary things?

4. Name some ways unforgiveness is fear based.

5. How does forgiveness make you stronger, not weaker?

Chapter Nine: Back on the Scene

1. What are some giants you fear?

2. Describe a situation in your life when you caved to fear and worshiped it.

3. Describe a situation in your life when you didn't cave to fear and trusted God instead.

4. Why do you think so many people focus on the worst-case scenarios instead of the best-case scenarios?

Chapter Ten: The Burn

1. What would you consider one of your burn experiences?

2. How has God revealed for you the truth about your burn?

3. Explain how God walks with you in your grief or pain or recovery.

4. When have you felt God's desire just to be near you, no strings attached?

5. How has your father helped you see God as a loving heavenly Father? How has your relationship with your father hindered your ability to see God as a loving heavenly Father?

Chapter Eleven: Finally at Home

1. How does fear keep you from doing a beautiful thing for Jesus with your life?

2. How does your fear emasculate God, stripping him of his dignity?

3. How does your fear keep you from intimacy with God?

4. What is the difference between how God thinks of your fears and how you think of your fears?

5. What specific verse could you begin to pray over your life?

Epilogue: Because of a Tree

1. How would you answer God if he swooped down right now and asked, "Where are you?"

2. How does fear shove you toward shame and away from God?

3. What are some first steps in tending the hope that God has placed inside your spirit?

Notes

Introduction: The Invitation

1. "I know the plans I have for you, says the Lord. They are plans for good and not for evil, to give you a future and a hope" (Jeremiah 29:11, TLB).
2. Mark 1:1 (NLT 1996).

Chapter 1: On the Curb

1. "So she called the name of the LORD who spoke to her, 'You are a God of seeing,' for she said, 'Truly here I have seen him who looks after me'" (Genesis 16:13, ESV).
2. "Yes, the LORD pours down his blessings" (Psalm 85:12).

Chapter 2: Promises

1. "This is how much God loved the world: He gave his Son, his one and only Son. And this is why: so that no one need be destroyed; by believing in him, anyone can have a whole and lasting life. God didn't go to all the trouble of sending his Son merely to point an accusing finger, telling the world how bad it was. He came to help, to put the world right again" (John 3:16–17, MSG).

2. "Just as you cannot understand the path of the wind or the mystery of a tiny baby growing in its mother's womb, so you cannot understand the activity of God, who does all things" (Ecclesiastes 11:5).

3. "'For I know the plans I have for you,' says the Lord. 'They are plans for good and not for disaster, to give you a future and a hope'" (Jeremiah 29:11).

4. "At about three o'clock, Jesus called out with a loud voice, *'Eli, Eli, lema sabachthani?'* which means 'My God, my God, why have you abandoned me?'" (Matthew 27:46).

5. "I have told you all this so that you may have peace in me. Here on earth you will have many trials and sorrows. But take heart, because I have overcome the world" (John 16:33).

6. "I will give them a heart to know Me, for I am the LORD; and they will be My people, and I will be their God, for they will return to Me with their whole heart" (Jeremiah 24:7, NASB).

Chapter 3: The Losing Team

1. "There is no fear in love, but perfect love casts out fear. For fear has to do with punishment, and whoever fears has not been perfected in love" (1 John 4:18, ESV).

2. "We know that God causes all things to work together for good to those who love God, to those who are called according to His purpose" (Romans 8:28, NASB).

3. "Then it goes and takes along seven other spirits more evil than itself, and they go in and live there; and the last state of that man becomes worse than the first" (Luke 11:26, NASB).

4. "He said to them, 'Why are you afraid? Do you still have no faith?'" (Mark 4:40, NASB).

5. "Then Jesus came with them to a place called Gethsemane, and said to His disciples, 'Sit here while I go over there and pray.' And He took with Him Peter and the two sons of Zebedee, and began to be grieved and distressed. Then He said to them, 'My soul is deeply grieved, to the point of death; remain here and keep watch with Me.'

   "And He went a little beyond them, and fell on His face and prayed, saying, 'My Father, if it is possible, let this cup pass from Me; yet not as I will, but as You will'" (Matthew 26:36–39, NASB).

6. "To bestow on them a crown of beauty instead of ashes, the oil of joy instead of mourning, and a garment of praise instead of a spirit of despair. They will be called oaks of righteousness, a planting of the LORD for the display of his splendor" (Isaiah 61:3, NIV).

7. "So Jacob was left alone, and a man wrestled with him till daybreak. When the man saw that he could not overpower him, he touched the socket of Jacob's hip so that his hip was wrenched as he wrestled with the man. Then the man said, 'Let me go, for it is daybreak.'

   "But Jacob replied, 'I will not let you go unless you bless me.'

   "The man asked him, 'What is your name?'

   "'Jacob,' he answered.

   "Then the man said, 'Your name will no longer be Jacob, but Israel, because you have struggled with God and with humans and have overcome'" (Genesis 32:24–28, NIV).

8. Numbers 13:27.

9. Numbers 13.

10. "'All right, you may test him,' the LORD said to Satan. 'Do whatever you want with everything he possesses, but don't harm him physically.' So Satan left the LORD's presence" (Job 1:12).

11. "It is in vain that you rise up early and go late to rest, eating the bread of anxious toil; for he gives to his beloved sleep" (Psalm 127:2, ESV).

12. "It is impossible to please God without faith. Anyone who wants to come to him must believe that God exists and that he rewards those who sincerely seek him" (Hebrews 11:6).

13. John Eldredge, *Walking with God: Talk to Him. Hear from Him. Really.* (Nashville: Thomas Nelson, 2008), 98.

14. Eldredge, *Walking with God,* 98.

Chapter 4: Easy Prey

1. "Jesus responded, 'Why are you afraid? You have so little faith!' Then he got up and rebuked the wind and waves, and suddenly there was a great calm" (Matthew 8:26).

2. "See, I have engraved you on the palms of my hands; your walls are ever before me" (Isaiah 49:16, NIV).

3. "Lord, through all the generations you have been our home!" (Psalm 90:1).

4. 1 Peter 5:8 (NIV 1984).

5. "I lie down and sleep; I wake again, because the LORD sustains me" (Psalm 3:5, NIV).

6. "The word of God is living and active, sharper than any two-edged sword, piercing to the division of soul and of spirit, of joints and of marrow, and discerning the thoughts and intentions of the heart" (Hebrews 4:12, ESV).

7. Isaiah 54:5.

Chapter 5: Close to the Cradle

1. Michael Leunig, *The Prayer Tree* (New York: Harper-Collins, 1992), introduction.

2. Brennan Manning, *All Is Grace: A Ragamuffin Memoir* (Colorado Springs: David C Cook, 2011), 106.

3. "One who was there had been an invalid for thirty-eight years. When Jesus saw him lying there and learned that he had been in this condition for a long time, he asked him, 'Do you want to get well?'

"'Sir,' the invalid replied, 'I have no one to help me into the pool when the water is stirred. While I am trying to get in, someone else goes down ahead of me.'

"Then Jesus said to him, 'Get up! Pick up your mat and walk.' At once the man was cured; he picked up his mat and walked" (John 5:5–9, NIV).

4. Leunig, *The Prayer Tree,* introduction.

Chapter 6: Flat on the Floor

1. Psalm 22:1–3, NLT 1996, emphasis added.

2. "But it happened that as I was on my way, approaching Damascus about noontime, a very bright light suddenly flashed from heaven all around me, and I fell to the ground and heard a voice saying to me, 'Saul, Saul, why are you persecuting Me?' And I answered, 'Who are You, Lord?' And He said to me, 'I am Jesus the Nazarene, whom you are persecuting.' And those who were with me saw the light, to be sure, but did not understand the voice of the One who was speaking to me. And I said, 'What

shall I do, Lord?' And the Lord said to me, 'Get up and go on into Damascus, and there you will be told of all that has been appointed for you to do.' But since I could not see because of the brightness of that light, I was led by the hand by those who were with me and came into Damascus" (Acts 22:6–11, NASB).

3. John Gill, "Acts 9, Gill's Exposition," Bible Hub, http://biblehub.com/commentaries/gill/acts/9.htm.

Chapter 7: Crying Out Loud

1. Brené Brown, PhD, LMSW, is an American scholar, author, and public speaker who is currently a research professor at the University of Houston Graduate College of Social Work.

2. Brené Brown, *Daring Greatly: How the Courage to Be Vulnerable Transforms the Way We Live, Love, Parent, and Lead* (New York: Gotham Books, 2012), 39.

3. Matthew 26:36–40 (NASB).

4. "As the time approached for him to be taken up to heaven, Jesus resolutely set out for Jerusalem" (Luke 9:51, NIV).

5. John Gill, "Luke 9:51," *Gill's Exposition of the Entire Bible,* Bible Study Tools, www.biblestudytools.com/commentaries/gills-exposition-of-the-bible/luke-9-51.html.

6. Matthew 5:3–4.

7. "Be strong and courageous. Do not fear or be in dread of them, for it is the LORD your God who goes with you. He will not leave you or forsake you" (Deuteronomy 31:6, ESV).

8. "You keep track of all my sorrows. You have collected all my tears in your bottle. You have recorded each one in your book" (Psalm 56:8).

9. "Let us not neglect our meeting together, as some people do, but encourage one another, especially now that the day of his return is drawing near" (Hebrews 10:25).

10. Job 7:20.

11. "If I have sinned, what have I done to you, O watcher of all humanity? Why make me your target? Am I a burden to you?" (Job 7:20).

12. Mother Teresa, *Mother Teresa: Come Be My Light,* ed. Brian Kolodiejchuk (New York: Doubleday, 2007), 165.

Chapter 8: A Big Misunderstanding

1. Penny & Sparrow, "Honest Wage," www.pennyandsparrow.com. Used by permission.

2. Luke 15:11–32, MSG.

3. Robert Lowry, "Nothing but the Blood of Jesus," 1876, public domain.

4. Ephesians 4:26–27, NASB.

5. "Then Abishai said to David, 'Today God has delivered

your enemy into your hand; now therefore, please let me strike him with the spear to the ground with one stroke, and I will not strike him the second time.' But David said to Abishai, 'Do not destroy him, for who can stretch out his hand against the LORD's anointed and be without guilt?' David also said, 'As the LORD lives, surely the LORD will strike him, or his day will come that he dies, or he will go down into battle and perish'" (1 Samuel 26:8–10, NASB).

Chapter 9: Back on the Scene

1. Matthew 2:11 (KJV).
2. Weymouth New Testament
3. Luke 22:42 (NIV).
4. "When Moses sent them to spy out the land of Canaan, he said to them, 'Go up there into the Negev; then go up into the hill country. See what the land is like, and whether the people who live in it are strong or weak, whether they are few or many. How is the land in which they live, is it good or bad? And how are the cities in which they live, are they like open camps or with fortifications? How is the land, is it fat or lean? Are there trees in it or not? Make an effort then to get some of the fruit of the land.' Now the time was the time of the first ripe grapes" (Numbers 13:17–20, NASB).

5. Numbers 13:27–29 (NASB).

6. "My servant Caleb, because he has had a different spirit and has followed Me fully, I will bring into the land which he entered, and his descendants shall take possession of it" (Numbers 14:24, NASB).

7. "Then Caleb quieted the people before Moses and said, 'We should by all means go up and take possession of it, for we will surely overcome it'" (Numbers 13:30, NASB).

8. "But because my servant Caleb has a different spirit and follows me wholeheartedly, I will bring him into the land he went to, and his descendants will inherit it" (Numbers 14:24, NIV).

9. "Your children will be shepherds here for forty years, suffering for your unfaithfulness, until the last of your bodies lies in the wilderness" (Numbers 14:33, NIV).

10. "Casting down imaginations, and every high thing that exalteth itself against the knowledge of God, and bringing into captivity every thought to the obedience of Christ" (2 Corinthians 10:5, KJV).

11. "Therefore, put on every piece of God's armor so you will be able to resist the enemy in the time of evil. Then after the battle you will still be standing firm. Stand your ground, putting on the belt of truth and the body armor of God's righteousness. For shoes, put on the peace that comes from the Good News so that you will be fully

prepared. In addition to all of these, hold up the shield of faith to stop the fiery arrows of the devil" (Ephesians 6:13–16).

12. 2 Corinthians 10:5 (NIV 1984).

13. Shauna Niequist, *Bittersweet: Thoughts on Change, Grace, and Learning the Hard Way* (Grand Rapids: Zondervan, 2010), 92–93.

Chapter 10: The Burn

1. "In the year that King Uzziah died, I saw the Lord, high and exalted, seated on a throne; and the train of his robe filled the temple. Above him were seraphim, each with six wings: With two wings they covered their faces, with two they covered their feet, and with two they were flying. And they were calling to one another: 'Holy, holy, holy is the LORD Almighty; the whole earth is full of his glory'" (Isaiah 6:1–3, NIV).

2. "He will not crush those who are weak or quench the smallest hope" (Isaiah 42:3, NLT 1996).

3. "A woman who had had a hemorrhage for twelve years, and had endured much at the hands of many physicians, and had spent all that she had and was not helped at all, but rather had grown worse—after hearing about Jesus, she came up in the crowd behind Him and touched His cloak. For she thought, 'If I just touch His garments, I

will get well.' Immediately the flow of her blood was dried up; and she felt in her body that she was healed of her affliction. Immediately Jesus, perceiving in Himself that the power proceeding from Him had gone forth, turned around in the crowd and said, 'Who touched My garments?' And His disciples said to Him, 'You see the crowd pressing in on You, and You say, "Who touched Me?"' And He looked around to see the woman who had done this. But the woman fearing and trembling, aware of what had happened to her, came and fell down before Him and told Him the whole truth. And He said to her, 'Daughter, your faith has made you well; go in peace and be healed of your affliction'" (Mark 5:25–34, NASB).

4. "Every good gift and every perfect gift is from above, coming down from the Father of lights with whom there is no variation or shadow due to change" (James 1:17, ESV).

5. "Assyria cannot save us; we will not mount warhorses. We will never again say 'Our gods' to what our own hands have made, for in you the fatherless find compassion" (Hosea 14:3, NIV).

6. "One cried unto another, and said, Holy, holy, holy, is the LORD of hosts: the whole earth is full of his glory" (Isaiah 6:3, KJV).

Chapter 11: Finally at Home

1. "Blessed are your eyes because they see, and your ears because they hear" (Matthew 13:16, NIV).

2. "Now when Jesus was at Bethany in the house of Simon the leper, a woman came up to him with an alabaster flask of very expensive ointment, and she poured it on his head as he reclined at table. And when the disciples saw it, they were indignant, saying, 'Why this waste? For this could have been sold for a large sum and given to the poor.' But Jesus, aware of this, said to them, 'Why do you trouble the woman? For she has done a beautiful thing to me. For you always have the poor with you, but you will not always have me. In pouring this ointment on my body, she has done it to prepare me for burial. Truly, I say to you, wherever this gospel is proclaimed in the whole world, what she has done will also be told in memory of her'" (Matthew 26:6–13, ESV).

3. Luke 7:37.

4. "She is clothed with strength and dignity, and she laughs without fear of the future" (Proverbs 31:25).

5. "When Abram was ninety-nine years old, the LORD appeared to him and said, 'I am God Almighty; walk before me faithfully and be blameless. Then I will make my covenant between me and you and will greatly increase your numbers.'

"Abram fell facedown, and God said to him, 'As for me, this is my covenant with you: You will be the father of many nations. No longer will you be called Abram; your name will be Abraham, for I have made you a father of many nations. I will make you very fruitful; I will make nations of you, and kings will come from you. I will establish my covenant as an everlasting covenant between me and you and your descendants after you for the generations to come, to be your God and the God of your descendants after you. The whole land of Canaan, where you now reside as a foreigner, I will give as an everlasting possession to you and your descendants after you; and I will be their God'" (Genesis 17:1–8, NIV).

6. "Therefore, say to the Israelites: 'I am the LORD, and I will bring you out from under the yoke of the Egyptians. I will free you from being slaves to them, and I will redeem you with an outstretched arm and with mighty acts of judgment. I will take you as my own people, and I will be your God. Then you will know that I am the LORD your God, who brought you out from under the yoke of the Egyptians. And I will bring you to the land I swore with uplifted hand to give to Abraham, to Isaac and to Jacob. I will give it to you as a possession. I am the LORD'" (Exodus 6:6–8, NIV).

7. "When your days are over and you rest with your ancestors, I will raise up your offspring to succeed you, your own flesh and blood, and I will establish his kingdom. He is the one who will build a house for my Name, and I will establish the throne of his kingdom forever" (2 Samuel 7:12–13, NIV).

8. "I remain confident of this: I will see the goodness of the LORD in the land of the living" (Psalm 27:13, NIV).

9. "God delivers me and exalts me; God is my strong protector and my shelter. Trust in him at all times, you people! Pour out your hearts before him! God is our shelter!" (Psalm 62:7–8, NET).

10. "All right then, the Lord himself will give you the sign. Look! The virgin will conceive a child! She will give birth to a son and will call him Immanuel (which means 'God is with us')" (Isaiah 7:14).

11. "Lord, through all the generations you have been our home!" (Psalm 90:1).

Epilogue: Because of a Tree

1. "The serpent was the shrewdest of all the wild animals the LORD God had made. One day he asked the woman, 'Did God really say you must not eat the fruit from any of the trees in the garden?'

"'Of course we may eat fruit from the trees in the garden,' the woman replied. 'It's only the fruit from the tree in the middle of the garden that we are not allowed to eat. God said, "You must not eat it or even touch it; if you do, you will die."'

"'You won't die!' the serpent replied to the woman. 'God knows that your eyes will be opened as soon as you eat it, and you will be like God, knowing both good and evil.'

"The woman was convinced. She saw that the tree was beautiful and its fruit looked delicious, and she wanted the wisdom it would give her. So she took some of the fruit and ate it. Then she gave some to her husband, who was with her, and he ate it, too. At that moment their eyes were opened, and they suddenly felt shame at their nakedness. So they sewed fig leaves together to cover themselves.

"When the cool evening breezes were blowing, the man and his wife heard the LORD God walking about in the garden. So they hid from the LORD God among the trees. Then the LORD God called to the man, 'Where are you?'" (Genesis 3:1–9).

2. Romans 8:1 (ESV).

3. "Grow in the grace and knowledge of our Lord and Savior Jesus Christ. To him be the glory both now and to the day of eternity. Amen" (2 Peter 3:18, ESV).

4. "I can do everything through Christ, who gives me strength" (Philippians 4:13).

5. "The LORD God placed the man in the Garden of Eden to tend and watch over it" (Genesis 2:15).

6. "I will lie down in peace and sleep, for you alone, O LORD, will keep me safe" (Psalm 4:8, NLT 1996).

7. "To all who mourn in Israel, he will give beauty for ashes, joy instead of mourning, praise instead of despair. For the LORD has planted them like strong and graceful oaks for his own glory" (Isaiah 61:3, NLT 1996).

8. "Publish his glorious deeds among the nations. Tell everyone about the amazing things he does" (Psalm 96:3, NLT 1996).

9. "I will tell everyone about your righteousness. All day long I will proclaim your saving power, for I am overwhelmed by how much you have done for me. I will praise your mighty deeds, O Sovereign LORD. I will tell everyone that you alone are just and good. O God, you have taught me from my earliest childhood, and I have constantly told others about the wonderful things you do. Now that I am old and gray, do not abandon me, O God. Let me proclaim your power to this new generation, your mighty miracles to all who come after me" (Psalm 71:15–18, NLT 1996).

10. "You are good and do only good; teach me your principles" (Psalm 119:68, NLT 1996).

11. "O my people, listen to my teaching. Open your ears to what I am saying, for I will speak to you in a parable. I will teach you hidden lessons from our past—stories we have heard and know, stories our ancestors handed down to us. We will not hide these truths from our children but will tell the next generation about the glorious deeds of the LORD. We will tell of his power and the mighty miracles he did" (Psalm 78:1–4, NLT 1996).

12. "How amazing are the deeds of the LORD! All who delight in him should ponder them" (Psalm 111:2, NLT 1996).

Acknowledgments

For my husband, Will. You love me and continue to pray for me, come what may. Thank you for believing God's promise that I would be clothed with strength and dignity and would laugh at the days to come.

My children: Will III and Amy, Emily and Kenton, and Sara. I love y'all, and I'm so grateful God made us into a family. And, hey, remember that stormy day in Estes Park when I got the call from Esther and found out God said yes to this story after decades of prayers? Glad you're always right there beside me.

My mom. We should all strive to be more like Mimi. Thank you for being a stronghold of peace, kindness, and love my whole life. And thank you for modeling what it means to be a God-honoring wife and mother. I love you.

My agent, Esther Fedorkovich. Thank you for believing in me as a writer and for securing a home for me and this story at WaterBrook Multnomah. I am so grateful for your perseverance. I wouldn't be here without you.

My editors, Laura Barker and Susan Tjaden. Thank you for pushing me and putting up with me. Thanks for all the phone calls, e-mails, and texts. This book wouldn't be what it is today without your patience and insight.

Carol Bartley, my production editor. Thank you for shepherding the grammar rule breaker in me and for making my words shine appropriately.

Ronne Rock. I am most thankful for the day at the lake house sorting out my lifeline, which just happened to turn into a finished proposal.

Hilliary Cheatham. Thank you for a sticky wall full of author notes, tears over gum drawers, and a beautiful front door with windows. You know I love you as if you were my own.

My readers group: Amanda Sherman, Hayley Morgan, Jessi Connolly, Ronne Rock, Chelsea Landis, and Bethany Stephens. Thank you for your thoughtful input and your vulnerable reflections. By God's grace we're all former fear-ers, yes?

And, finally, the team at WaterBrook Multnomah. Thank you for your care, encouragement, and hard work.